How children learn - Book 2

by Linda Pound

Contents

Published by Step Forward Publishing Limited
St Jude's Church, Dulwich Road, Herne Hill, London, SE24 0PB
Tel: 020 7738 5454

www.practicalpreschool.com

Illustrations: Cathy Hughes

Introduction

This book, a sequel to How Children Learn, shares many of its features. It also attempts to explain a range of theories about children's learning. It seeks to promote the reflective practice which is a vital characteristic of professionalism. It sets out to encourage you to think about why you do what you do in your important work with children.

As we saw in *How Children Learn*, theories can be developed from research and experimentation or they may be drawn from philosophy or hypothetical ideas. Whatever their basis, the importance of observation is a common strand. All the theories explored in this book were developed by theorists who observed how people, including children, learn.

In the first book, the focus was largely on individual theorists (such as Lev Vygotsky and Margaret Donaldson). In addition, there were some sections dedicated to renowned educational movements (such as High/Scope and Te Whariki) or important elements of education and learning (such as brain development, emotional intelligence and learning through play). In this, the second book, the central theme remains children's learning, but there is an attempt to focus more firmly on trends and developments rather than individual theorists. It looks, for example, at the way in which ancient theories of learning both in the classical world and the east have shaped current views about the way in which children learn. It also considers the way in which ideas about how children learn to read and talk have developed and changed over time.

This underlines the way in which theories change. Each theorist builds on other people's ideas. This can be seen, for example, in considering the way in which theories about creativity have developed over time. In many sections the impact of the social and political context can be seen. With the development of each new theory, understanding grows and changes.

About this book

• As far as possible, the order in which theories have developed and evolved is reflected in the order in which they are presented within each section. You should not assume from this that as new theories develop, the others fade away. As was shown in *How Children Learn*, Skinner's behaviourist theories were developed later than Piaget's. This did not mean however that behaviourism demolished Piaget's ideas of the child as a scientist, constructing knowledge. Far from it. In fact, Piaget's theories continue to be more influential than those of Skinner among theorists. Skinner's behaviourist theory is widely regarded as too simplistic to explain human behaviour. On the other hand, in many aspects of life behaviourism remains the basis of how adults approach children's learning. If you have heard yourself saying to a child, 'if you eat your peas, you can have a sweet' you have been making use of behaviourist theory.

• Most sections follow a similar format. Key dates and key figures are identified and a concluding comment section draws some conclusions. The section on the ancient theories of Socrates, Plato, Aristotle and Confucius has a slightly different shape since it is looking at their work individually. In this case, a comment section makes some reference to the impact of their work as a whole.

- You will find many connections both with the theories outlined in *How Children Learn* and with other sections of this book. Any such links are highlighted in order to help you explore the connections which will help you to understand and make sense of these complex ideas. The many overlaps and connections which you will find remind us that good ideas do not emerge from just one person but that human thinking links with other thinking. It also links with events and issues which constantly face us. So, for example, in several sections you will notice the impact of war on society's view of what education is for.

- This book covers vast areas of theory and understanding. This means that it can be no more than a brief introduction to the ideas explored, designed to whet your appetite so that you want to find out more for yourself. Most importantly, the book aims to encourage you to link these theories to your observations of children so that you can better analyse and understand how children learn.

Note to students:

Every effort has been made to make sure that you have all the information you will need to cite sources in your essays and projects. You will need to rearrange these references in your written work in order to meet the demands of tutors and accreditation bodies. Before you hand in your assignments, double check that you have met the requirements of your particular course or place of study.

There is guidance in each section to help you track down further information for yourself. The information in this book is by no means the end of the story. There is much more to be read, discussed and learned from the work of the remarkable figures introduced in these pages. Because the book often takes an historical overview, some of the books referred to are no longer in print. This means that you should check with your library to see whether they can help you to access some of these texts.

Two words of warning:

Be very careful about accurate referencing – your written work should include a reference to all sources that you have used in your written work. Carelessness could lead to you being accused of plagiarism – a very serious matter.

Secondly, use websites with caution. Some offer excellent information, others offer misleading, incomplete or simply wrong information. Always think about who has published the information and what their motive might be.

Any website addresses provided were valid at the time of going to press.

Ancient theories that shaped modern thinking about learning

The work of Greek philosophers, stretching back thousands of years, has had an impact on our understanding of learning and teaching, and the ways in which we can support learning. In the east, the work of Confucius has had an equally strong impact. This section examines some of the ways in which their ideas, stretching back more than two thousand years, continue to influence educational thinking.

Although there are many complex arguments and ideas in this section, it is worth persevering because they have had such a strong influence on current thinking about what learning involves and how it is best supported. As indicated in the introduction to this book, the format of this section is a little different to that of subsequent sections. This is because it focuses on the theories of individuals, just drawing them together at the end of the section. Subsequent sections focus on trends and developments across theories.

East meets west

The names of Socrates, Plato and Aristotle, if not their ideas, have become household words. Although we may never consciously think of them as we go about our daily lives, it is widely argued that it was their inquiry into the nature of knowledge which has been the foundation for all subsequent philosophical thinking. The American poet W.H. Auden has suggested that if Greek civilization had not developed philosophy as it did 'we would never have become fully conscious, which is to say that we would never have become, for better or worse, fully human' (1).

This view, however, ignores the huge impact of eastern philosophers on large sections of the world beyond Europe. The name of an eastern philosopher, Confucius, is today just as familiar to us as those of the Greek philosophers mentioned above. Confucius is frequently referred to in western society in a humorous fashion, references to him usually beginning with the phrase 'Confucius he say...'. However, as with references to the Greek philosophers, working at a similar time in history, most people know little of what he actually thought (or said) or what his influence has been on the way in which practitioners today try to support children's learning.

Many present day writers (2) suggest that these and other ancient philosophers continue to have a significant influence on the way in which people around the world think and learn. Moreover, they believe that the contrasting philosophies of the ancient worlds of east and west have had an impact in shaping the thinking and learning favoured in those parts of the world.

Socrates

His life

Socrates was born in the middle of the fifth century BC. The exact date is not really known. He has been described as the most noble and wisest Athenian ever, but less flatteringly as snub-nosed, prematurely bald, and overweight. His method of teaching led some people to think of him as ill-tempered, perhaps because he challenged his students to think for themselves. It is believed that his father was a stone cutter and his mother a midwife. Rather like Jean-Jacques Rousseau hundreds of years later in the eighteenth century (see *How Children Learn* pages 6-7), Socrates is said to have neglected his family. He dedicated himself to the education of young Athenian men, throwing himself into the intellectual life of debate and discussion which he loved. In this process, his wife and three sons were condemned to a life of relative poverty.

Although much has been written about the Greeks' 'remarkable sense of personal agency – the sense that they were in charge of their own lives and free to act as they chose' (3), it was Socrates' questioning of Athenian values, laws, customs, and religion which led to his trial and subsequent execution in 399 BC. He was found guilty of treason to the gods and was sentenced to death. In the writings of his most famous student, Plato, we learn that Socrates was charged with curiosity. Wanting to know more about everything was seen as an evil act, as was his additional crime of talking to others about his ideas.

Many other people whose lives at that time were similarly threatened, simply fled the country, something which Socrates' friends and supporters urged him to do, but he chose to remain in Athens. He was only found guilty by a slim majority of the council and was offered the option of paying a fine. He chose, however, to take the punishment of drinking hemlock. His calm acceptance of death is said to have made him a model for other philosophers to follow.

His writing

Socrates himself wrote nothing. His major philosophical theories were written down by his best known student, Plato (with the help of his friend Xenaphon).

His theory and influence

It would be difficult to overestimate the influence which Socrates' thinking has had on our understanding of and approach to learning and teaching throughout the last two thousand years. He has been described as the father of philosophy – which is sometimes defined as belief, or the search for wisdom.

He, like many other Athenians of the time, was curious about the world around him and the nature of learning. He explored a wide variety of philosophical questions. He was probably the first philosopher to make a clear distinction between the body and soul, placing a higher value on the soul. It has been said that Socrates was remarkable for living the life he preached. This is true in some ways – he did not for example charge fees, but merely started and extended philosophical arguments wherever young and intelligent men would listen. Young men flocked to his side clinging to his every word and asking his advice about practical conduct and educational problems. He did not reveal answers or claim to know the truth. Many of his questions were, on the surface, quite simple: such as 'what is courage?'; 'what is virtue?'; 'what is duty?' Through discussion his students came to discover how complex these subjects were.

Plato

His life

Plato, one of the most famous Greek philosophers, was, like Socrates, born in Athens. His mother was Pericione, and his father's name was Ariston. After the premature death of his father, his mother married one of his uncles. Another uncle and a cousin subsequently became dictators of Athens and invited Plato to join them. He declined because he disapproved of their practices which he claimed were cruel and unethical. In 403 BC, democracy was restored to Athens but the execution of his friend and teacher, Socrates, led him to leave Athens disillusioned.

Plato returned to Athens in 387 BC, and founded a school of philosophy. He himself was regarded as a master of geometry. The school was called the Academy, considered by many to be the first ever university. The school was to remain open for almost 900 years. It was closed down in AD 529 by Justinian, the Byzantine emperor.

His writing

Plato wrote over thirty dialogues which in the main presented Socrates' most important ideas. However, his greatest and most enduring work was his lengthy dialogue, *The Republic*. This dialogue discusses the education necessary to produce the society he regarded as an ideal one – an holistic education giving equal importance to physical, mental and spiritual development.

He described his ideal society as one which would not be a democracy but which would be ruled by a Philosopher-King. The aim of his book *The Republic* was to warn all Athenians that without respect for law, leadership and a high quality of education for the young, their city would continue to decay. For him, the Philosopher-Kings which he proposed would restore Athens to its former status.

His theory and influence

Plato's writing in *The Republic* outlines his theory of knowledge. Like Socrates, Plato asks philosophical questions such as: 'what is knowledge?'; 'what is illusion?', 'what is reality and how do we know?'

These are not dissimilar to the kinds of questions – known as epistemological questions – which, two thousand years later, Piaget was asking (see *How Children Learn* page 36–38). They are questions about knowledge itself. As Piaget was to believe so many years later, Plato developed a belief or theory

PROFILE

Plato was Socrates' most famous student and he wrote all that is now known of Socrates' teaching and philosophy.

KEY DATES

427 BC
born

387 BC
established a school in Athens

360 BC
publication of The Republic

347 BC
died

LINKS

- Socrates
- Aristotle

that knowledge is particular to or constructed by each individual. For him, reality was always changing and relied on the senses – sight, touch, taste, sound and smell. (Incidentally, these five senses were defined by Socrates for the first time ever all those years ago.) Building on the ideas of Socrates, Plato argued that reality is known only through the mind. However he also believed in a higher world, independent of the world of our senses, which can mislead us. This higher world is unchanging, absolute and universal. He believed that art or beauty should form the basis of education (4).

'It is surely one of the curiosities of the history of philosophy that one of the most cherished notions of this great man has never been taken seriously by any of his followers.... Scholars have played with his thesis as with a toy: they have acknowledged its beauty, its logic, its completeness; but never for a moment have they considered its feasibility. They have treated Plato's most passionate ideal as an idle paradox, only to be understood in the context of a lost civilization.' (5)

Plato's theory of education relies on what is known as Socratic dialogue. A Socratic dialogue takes the form of question-answer, question-answer, question-answer. Like a debate. Socrates would argue both sides of a question in order to arrive at a conclusion. Then that conclusion would be argued against another assumption, and so on.

One of the areas in which Plato built on Socrates' views is in his belief that mankind is born with knowledge. He claimed, for example, in an approach known as Platonic argument, that we cannot learn about squares or triangles from sensory experience but that the knowledge is recollected or already present in our minds. This may explain why Socrates did not give his students answers, but only questions. His job was not to teach truth but to enable students to reveal the truth they already knew. Only in conversation or dialogue, both Socrates and Plato believed, can truth and wisdom come to the surface.

Plato's ideas were in many ways forward looking – he argued that women should have the same opportunities for education as men (6) – a remarkable view for that time.

Aristotle

His life

Aristotle was born in Stagira but because his parents died young he was brought up by a man named Proxemus. His father had been a physician. At the age of eighteen, Aristotle became a student at the university established by Plato, the Academy, where he subsequently was to become Plato's most famous student. Aristotle regarded himself a biologist but he was well versed in and able to teach a wide range of subjects, including astronomy, physics, logic, aesthetics, music, drama, tragedy, poetry, zoology, ethics and politics. Unlike his teacher Plato, the one field in which he did not excel was mathematics.

The King of Macedonia asked Aristotle to supervise the education of his son, Alexander, who later conquered Greece and became known as Alexander the Great. In 334 BC Aristotle founded a school of philosophy known as the Lyceum, in Athens. Like Plato's Academy, it too was closed by Justinian in AD 529.

After Alexander the Great died in 323 BC, Aristotle, like Socrates before him, was charged by the Athenian people with impiety or a failure to offer due reverence to the gods. The Athenians resented his friendship with Alexander, who had conquered them. Unlike Socrates who had remained in Athens and accepted with equanimity the death sentence passed on him, Aristotle fled to Chalcis, where he died one year later in 322 BC.

His writing

Very little of Aristotle's writings remain extant. But his students recorded nearly everything he discussed at the Lyceum. In fact, the books to which Aristotle's name is attributed are really little more than student notebooks. This may account for the fact that Aristotle's philosophy is one of the more difficult to understand. However, Steven Pinker (7), an American psychologist who writes both accessibly and prolifically, reminds us that the fact that his ideas were written down at all should act as a constant reminder that 'it is a strange and thrilling thought that every time you refer to Aristotle, you are connected through a very long chain of speakers to the man himself'.

His theory and influence

Aristotle believed that curiosity was the uniquely defining characteristic of human beings. Plato's most famous student, Aristotle, was also among his fiercest critics. While Plato suggested that man was born with knowledge,

PROFILE

Just as Plato had been Socrates' student, so Aristotle was Plato's student. He was later to become tutor to Alexander the Great.

KEY DATES

384 BC
born

366 BC
entered Plato's Academy

343/2 BC
became tutor to Alexander the Great

334 BC
set up his own school

322 BC
died

LINKS

• Plato

Ancient theories that shaped modern thinking about learning

Aristotle argued that knowledge comes from experience. These two points of view have represented the essence of western intellectual and philosophical thinking since that time. Plato's view is known as Rationalism (in which knowledge comes before experience), whereas Aristotle's view that knowledge comes after experience is described as Empiricism.

Confucius

His life

Confucius, according to Chinese tradition, was a thinker, political figure and educator. It is difficult to separate fiction and fact in considering the life and work of Confucius. There are therefore many differing accounts of his life. Confucius (as he is known in the west) is properly known as Kong Qiu. Although born into an aristocratic family, his father died when Confucius was just three years old. His life after that was more impoverished than could have been expected for a family of that rank and his early employment included caring for livestock.

Confucius married at the age of nineteen. His mother died in 527 BC, and after a period of mourning he began his career as a teacher, opening his own school at about the age of thirty. After some political involvement and intrigue which led to his exile in 492 BC, Confucius returned to work in his own school which it is claimed had 3,000 students by the time of his death. It is thought that Confucius died at the age of seventy two. This is disputed by some who suggest that this is part of the mythology which surrounds Confucius' life and work. Seventy-two is regarded as a magic number of great significance in early Chinese literature and might therefore be claimed by some of his followers to underline his greatness. After Confucius died, he was buried in a grave in the city of Ch'uFu, Shandong. Today the site of his final resting place is the beautiful K'ung Forest, which continues to be a popular place for tourists.

His writing

Like Socrates, Confucius did not put into writing the principles of his philosophy; these were handed down only through his disciples. He is believed to have written a number of songs although the tunes are not written down.

The *Lun Yu*, a work compiled by some of his disciples, is considered the most reliable source of information about his life and teachings. One of the historical works that he is said to have compiled and edited is the *Ch'un Ch'iu* (Spring and Autumn Annals). This is an account of Chinese history in the state of Lu from 722 to 481 BC. His own teachings, together with those of his main disciples, are found in the Four Books of Confucian literature, known as *Shih Shu*, which became the textbooks of many later Chinese generations. Confucius did not regard it as his role to create learning, but rather to pass on the core values and teachings of society. He therefore revived the study of what were known as the ancient books.

PROFILE

A revered Chinese teacher and educator whose life and work is legendary in China and beyond, Confucius' influence in Chinese history has been compared to that of Socrates in the West.

KEY DATES

551 BC
born

532 BC
married

527 BC
his mother died

522 BC
established a school

502 BC
became an official in the Kingdom of Lu

501 BC
became Minister of Justice

492 BC
exiled

479 BC
died

His theory and influence

His fame as a man of learning and character and his reverence for Chinese ideals and customs soon spread through the principality of Lu. Confucius deplored the contemporary disorder and lack of moral standards and emphasised the value of the ancient values of Chinese society. He taught the great value of the power of example. Rulers, he said, can be great only if they themselves lead exemplary lives. He also believed in the importance of learning and education. It is believed that he said that 'those who excel in office should learn; those who excel in learning should take office' (8). Confucius' principles were drawn from the ancient traditions of Chinese culture. He emphasised family loyalties, ancestor worship, and respect for elders. He espoused what is known as the Golden Rule, often expressed as 'do unto others as you would be done by'. Confucius stressed the importance of long and careful study but regarded it as much more than book learning. Study, for him, meant finding a good teacher and imitating his words and deeds. Confucius expressed himself as willing to teach anyone who was willing to learn. Morality was the core of studies but he also focused on the 'Six Arts' – ritual, music, archery, chariot-riding, calligraphy, and computation. Like Socrates', Confucius' teaching relied on questions. In modern China, it is reported that families are now sending their children to weekend classes to learn the traditional ways of Confucius.

Putting the theories into practice

The views of Socrates, Plato and Aristotle have inspired many educationalists in the twentieth and the twenty-first centuries, notably John Dewey (*How Children Learn* pages 21–22) and Friedrich Froebel (*How Children Learn* pages 14–16). Their work is regarded as the basis of western philosophy – just as the work of Confucius is regarded as the foundation of eastern philosophy.

In Dewey's work, their influence is seen in the fact that he believed that human beings need science and democracy in order to flourish – both as individuals and as a society. He, like Aristotle, took an empiricist view believing that knowledge arises out of experience. He stated (9) for example that:

- Education is not preparation for life. Education is life itself
- Give the pupils something to do, not something to learn and the doing is of such a nature as to demand thinking; learning naturally results.

Froebel also believed in experience as the basis of knowledge. Moreover in his 'gifts' – the shaped blocks which children were given – he echoed the emphasis placed on beauty by the Greek philosophers. He, like them, regarded education as holistic rather than simply intellectual. He stressed that education must cater for children's physical, emotional, intellectual, social, aesthetic and spiritual development.

It is also interesting to note that Dewey's views have, in their turn, had a strong influence on current educational theories in China. Dewey spent some time there, from 1919–1921. Chen Heqin (1892–1982) had studied with Dewey at Columbia University during 1917 and 1918. Tao Xingzh won a scholarship to study in America in 1916 and subsequently met Dewey again when he travelled to China in 1919. They developed schools and teacher training. Tao Xingzh was able to adapt Dewey's philosophy arguing for:

- society as school (rather than school as society)
- life as education (rather than education as life), and
- unity of teaching, learning and reflective acting (rather than learning by doing).

Although there was a period when Dewey's ideas were vilified in China, the reality was that his views on democracy and moral persuasion were widely to be seen in practice. Today it is regarded as part of a national education reform movement – rather than simply an experiment. Tao, building on the ideals of Confucius, is regarded as a national hero, commended by Mao

Ancient theories that shaped modern thinking about learning

Zedong in 1988 as a great people's educator (10), and with a memorial hall in Shanghai marking his educational achievements.

Comment

Despite the links between theories arising out of ancient Greek philosophy and current practice in China, there remains a vast gap between eastern and western philosophies. A Chinese philosopher asked why he thought the east and the west had developed such different habits of thought answered 'because you had Aristotle and we had Confucius' (11).

The major difference between eastern and western modes of thought is fundamental. The dialogic style of teaching developed by Socrates led the Greeks to emphasise what has been described as logical discussion in which the aim is to demolish the arguments of those with whom you are discussing. Chinese thinking on the other hand has tended to emphasise collective thinking, in which the opinions of others are merged with your own – coming to a common understanding, in which neither is wholly right or wrong. This difference is even reflected in music where Chinese tradition is monophonic with everyone singing the same tune, while the Greeks developed polyphony with a number of individual parts being sung over one another (12).

We must, however, be careful not to assume that these cultural differences are unchanging or unchangeable. For example, studies carried out in the United States of America indicate that children born in the west of Chinese parentage are able to think and learn in ways that owe something to both traditions.

References

(1)   Auden, W. H. (1977) The Portable Greek Reader *Harmondsworth: Penguin Books*

(2)   Nisbett, R. (2003) The Geography of Thought *London: Nicholas Brealey Publishing*

(3)   Palmer, J. (ed) (2001) Fifty Major Thinkers on Education *London: Routledge*

(4)   Read, H. (1943) Education Through Art *London: Faber and Faber*

(5)   Read, H. (1943) Education Through Art *London: Faber and Faber (p.1)*

(6)   Cooper, D. (2001) 'Plato' in Palmer, J. (ed) Fifty Major Thinkers on Education: from Confucius to Dewey *London: Routledge*

(7)   Pinker, S. (2007) The Stuff of Thought *London: Allen Lane (p. 291)*

(8)   Shen, J. (2001) 'Confucius' in Palmer, J. (ed) Fifty Major Thinkers on Education: from Confucius to Dewey *London: Routledge (p. 2)*

(9)   Dewey, J. (1897) My Pedagogic Creed. School Journal 54: 77–80

Ancient theories that shaped modern thinking about learning

(10)   Teachers College (1997) *The China Connection. www.tc.edu/news/ article.htm?id=3793 accessed 23/2/08.*

(11)   Nisbett, R. (2003) The Geography of Thought *London: Nicholas Brealey Publishing (page 29)*

(12)   Nisbett, R. (2003) The Geography of Thought *London: Nicholas Brealey Publishing*

Where to find out more

Nisbett, R. (2003) The Geography of Thought *London: Nicholas Brealey Publishing*

Palmer, J. (ed) (2001) Fifty Major Thinkers on Education *London: Routledge*

The development of theories about how children learn to read and write

Developing theories

The introduction of new approaches can be seen to follow a clear pattern but this does not mean that all schools and all teachers either took up new methods or discarded old ones. All that can be firmly identified are emerging trends. Analysis of approaches in America suggested that in broad terms whole word (or look and say) methods were predominant from 1940–1970; phonic methods from 1970–1990; and whole language (or language experience) methods from 1990 onwards. In Britain phonic approaches (in particular what is known as synthetic phonics) are currently being strongly emphasised. However, it would be wrong to think that phonics teaching had ever disappeared.

The alphabetic method

Amongst the earliest known materials for teaching reading in this country are hornbooks (1), so named because the writing was protected by a thin sheet of animal horn. Hornbooks were probably introduced towards the end of the fourteenth century and included the letters of the alphabet shown in both upper and lower case and familiar prayers such as the Lord's Prayer. In this method children were taught the names of the letters and to recite them. Later, in the nineteenth and into the twentieth century, methods focused on the tactile approach of feeling the letter shapes by, for example, children tracing their fingers around sandpaper letters. To this day they are encouraged to play with magnetic and foam letters in order to become familiar with the shapes.

While the alphabetic method emphasises letter names (eg. 'C', 'A', 'T' spells cat), many practitioners today believe that children need to know letter names ('a' as in able) at the same time as they are being introduced to the sounds that they make ('a' as in cat). Research undertaken in the 1970s (2) suggested that children who appeared to learn to read without formal instruction at a very early age usually knew the names of the letters, but that this had come about as a result of learning to read, rather than as a preparation for it. It is also apparent that some children able to read fluently are not able to decipher decontextualized letters.

The beginnings of the phonics method

Phonics were introduced in the middle of the nineteenth century. The examples from early primers underline how tedious and meaningless this approach can be, but some children clearly did learn to read by this method. This example comes from a book published in 1913 (3):

1. is it in?
2. or is it on?
3. it is an ox
4. an ox is at it

Phonic reading schemes were introduced in the 1920s with the publication of Beacon Readers in 1922. By the 1940s and 1950s, many teachers had become disillusioned with phonics approaches and begun to move towards whole word and whole sentence methods.

Whole word methods

The focus on meaning which was developing from progressive approaches to education, particularly in the period between the two world wars and from the work of John Dewey (see *How Children Learn* pages 21–22), led to the introduction of a whole word method. Children were encouraged to focus on the shape of words in order to remember them. In addition they were introduced to words which were particularly interesting or important to children (such as their names or mum) or which had a distinctive shape (such as aeroplane or elephant).

One such approach, developed by Schonell, led to the introduction of a reading test which remained influential for many years. One hundred words beginning with tree, little, milk, egg, book, school, sit, frog, playing and bun and ending with metamorphosis, somnambulist, bibliography and idiosyncrasy were used to determine a child's reading age. Schonell suggests that (4) words are learnt through aural means (saying and hearing words); meaning; writing (physical reinforcement); and most importantly through the visual pattern.

Whole sentence methods

One important aspect of psychological thinking in this period is known as the Gestalt school of psychology. Their emphasis is on seeing things as a whole – suggesting that our brains make sense or meaning of things that are incomplete by making them whole. For example, in many cartoons a few carefully placed pen strokes will convey a particular image – our brains fill in the gaps. This theory led to whole sentence approaches to the teaching of reading. The rationale was that the context about which children were reading would help them to fill in the words they did not know. Advocates of this method would cite examples in which experienced readers skip over inaccuracies in print, often without even noticing them. Perhaps you've been caught out by sentences such as:

Flowers will bloom in the
the spring.

Criticisms of whole word and sentence methods

Whole word methods were generally taught through the use of flash cards, which did not fit comfortably with the more progressive methods of teaching which were being developed in the 1950s. Flash cards use a rote method of learning and rely on a behaviourist approach – such as Skinner used to train rats and pigeons (see *How Children Learn* pages 42–43). Children respond to the stimulus of the flash card being shown and learning is reinforced by the teacher's enthusiasm or praise (or perhaps punished by not collecting as many cards successfully read as other children in the group). The approaches were also seen as making children too dependent on adults – the only way to decipher an unknown word was, it was suggested, to ask the teacher.

The return of phonics methods

In the 1950s, Daniels and Diack introduced the Royal Road reading scheme. This scheme is still available but it has always been more used by older children having difficulties with reading than by young children in the early stages of learning to read. It focuses on what have come to be known as CVC (consonant-vowel-consonant) words such as tip, top, tap, tin, and tub.

This scheme or approach also led to a widely used reading test. Words such as on, in, hot, hat, jam and him are used and, based on the number of words children can correctly identify, they are given a reading age.

Research-based methods of learning to read

From the 1960s onwards a number of new approaches emerged. There was widespread dissatisfaction with existing methods creating a receptive audience for the range of new methods which began to emerge. The first two described below are probably the best known.

The Initial Teaching Alphabet

One of these innovative approaches was developed by Sir James Pitman and published in 1961. It was known as the Initial Teaching Alphabet (ITA) and was based on a new alphabet. Twenty-four of the existing twenty-six letters of the alphabet are used – omitting q and x. Twenty additional characters were added so that all the sounds of the English language could be individually represented. Although it is claimed that only 13% of English words do not use standard correspondence between sounds and letters, the main reason for developing this approach was to make spelling more systematic.

the ies ænjel gav ɟhe oul a rŋ

Can you read what this says? (5)

By the time the Bullock Report into reading was published in 1975, 9% of schools were using ITA. The expectation was that children and their parents would be able to read and write using ITA by the age of seven – at which point there was to be a gradual shift towards using standard spelling and letters.

Despite high levels of publicity, by the mid-1980s ITA had virtually disappeared. It is claimed that one of the reasons for this failure was that, at a time when the range and variety of children's books were growing, there were relatively few books published using ITA. A widely cited reason for its lack of success is the claim by many people who were introduced to ITA at the start of their schooling, that the transition to the standard alphabet was not without a number of difficulties. Many children appeared to have great difficulty in learning to spell in standard ways.

Solution to ITA text: The ice angel gave the owl a ring.

Key words
In 1968, a reading scheme was published by Ladybird, the publishers of a wide range of children's books. The series was based on research which identified the most commonly used words in the English language, drawing on children's and adult's books as well as children's speech. The authors claimed (6) that twelve words (a, and, he, I, in, is, it, of, that, the, to, was) make up over a quarter of the total number of words used in books and children's spoken language. These twelve words together with a further 88 words make up over half of such language. The next most frequently used twenty words include all, as, at, be, but, are, for, had, have, him, his, not, on, one, said, so, they, we, with, and you. As these are all very short words, without distinctive patterns, it is clear that children would not be able to rely on the visual patterns favoured by whole word methods. They are also almost entirely words without clear meaning – a little better than the 'it is an ox' of the early phonics methods (see previous section on alphabetic methods) but

still not exciting. Not many interesting sentences or phrases may be made up from these words that make up half of all we say and read.

Language experience and whole language approaches to reading

It is interesting to note that, despite their many differences, both Key Words and ITA were criticised for not paying sufficient attention to the natural patterns of language. In the 1970s, the Schools Council led research and consequently fostered an approach to reading which emphasised 'language-experience', involving a range of different methods. It was based on the following principles:

1. What children think about, they can talk about
2. What they can talk about can also be expressed in painting, writing,etc.
3. Anything they write can be read
4. They can read what they write and what other people write
5. In representing speech with symbols, the same symbols (letters) are used over and over again
6. Each letter in the alphabet stands for one or more of the sounds that are made in speech
7. Every word begins with a sound that can be written down
8. Most words have an ending sound
9. Many words have some sound(s) in between the beginning and ending sounds
10. Some words are used over and over again in English. (7)

Breakthrough to Literacy

These principles led, in part, to the publication of Breakthrough to Literacy, which consisted of a large teacher's folder containing word cards. The cards were selected and placed in a plastic stand, called a sentence maker. Children were given small versions of the teacher's folder and word cards added as children became able to read or recognise them. Children composed their own sentences on individual sentence makers. The folders were printed with a large number of words important in children's communication – nouns such as mum, television, baby, dad; verbs such as like and went; a variety of incidental words such as a, the, and; and adjectives like little and big.

Children were encouraged to create their own sentences from these words. They could use additional blank cards to collect their individual favourite words (such as the names of brothers and sisters or popular television characters). The underlying philosophy was that children should be encouraged to use their everyday language so that sentences which did not conform to standard English were accepted. So, for example, presented with a child's sentence which read 'My mum and dad is big', the teacher would allow that to stand – while modelling the standard English. This might mean that he or she would say to a child something like: '"My mum and dad is big." I like that sentence – your mummy and daddy are big aren't they? They're taller than you and taller than me.'

Breakthrough to Literacy also had a set of readers which used the same core vocabulary. In an effort to increase children's interest level, many schools began to band several reading schemes so that instead of simply working through the books of one scheme, children were encouraged to choose from books identified as having a similar level of difficulty. Cliff Moon introduced what he termed individualised reading – a booklet indicating the level of difficulty of a wide range of reading scheme books. (8).

Reading with real books
Despite the innovations described above, there was still widespread dissatisfaction with standards of reading. In 1979, Don Holdaway, an advocate of real books in New Zealand wrote (9):

Even in the most advanced societies schools have failed to achieve the 19th Century dream of a universally literate society. The dream may have been unrealistic or the goal even undesirable, but nothing in the educational world can match the resources of every kind that have been poured into this effort and, more recently, into the remediation of its countless failures. Should we not have sufficient clues from the broad span of research in learning, in human development, in linguistics, and in sociology to draw sound conclusions about this failure and its proper resolution?

The conclusion that Holdaway along with many other writers, researchers and theorists (such as Frank Smith, Kenneth Goodman and Donald Graves) came to was that reading, like many other complex skills, would be best learnt 'in natural environments without the support of highly trained professionals' (9). An approach to reading developed which drew on the 'whole language' approaches which had been developing, together with increased understanding of language and its development which led to what was known as reading with real books. The large number of beautiful picture books for young children which came onto the market during the 1960s and 1970s fostered the view that reading scheme books offered impoverished language and were of less interest to children. At first, schools used a wide variety of reading schemes in order to enrich children's experience, but over time scheme books were frequently replaced by children's story books. This was to become known as the real books approach to reading – distinguishing it from learning to read through a reading scheme.

Holdaway developed the use of big books, now widely used for large group and shared reading. He argued that their use gave children who did not enjoy the luxury of a bedtime story the opportunity to learn about how books and print work. Key principles in successful shared book experience include (10):

- the texts used need to be those which children enjoy
- the teacher needs to present new material with wholehearted enjoyment
- the ancient satisfactions of chant and song can be used to sustain the feelings of involvement among pupils
- teaching-learning sequences can be developed to revisit favourite poems, jingles, songs and stories; to attend to words, letters and sounds; to use a new story to model and explain word-solving strategies; to link shared reading to independent and group reading and writing.

Marie Clay (1926-2007) and Reading Recovery

Marie Clay, another New Zealander, shared many of Holdaway's views about books and print. She developed Reading Recover, which is an approach which offers one-to-one support to children who are experiencing reading difficulties. After one year in school, a diagnostic survey (which in New Zealand falls close to each child's sixth birthday) identifies those children most in need of this support. The support is carefully structured in order to develop in the children who are having the greatest difficulty 'behaviours which appear spontaneously in most children'. The ultimate aim is to make children independent readers, able to self-correct and use a range of what Clay calls 'self-improving strategies' (11).

Marie Clay has researched young children's reading behaviour extensively, like many others interested in naturalistic approaches to becoming literate. She encourages teachers to encourage children to use a variety of strategies in learning to read. These include visual cues (word and letter knowledge), language cues (guesses which focus on what kind of word is likely to be in the text) and spatial cues (is it a big or small word? Does it have a long tail or double o as in book and look?) She suggests that children look for a 'best-fit' solution and that a range of cues helps them to make the decision. Her emphasis on self-correction underlines her belief that by making mistakes children 'gradually become aware, at the level of conscious reasoning, of what they are doing, and able to verbalize this' (12).

She describes the reading behaviour of successful young readers as being like that of mature readers, and indicates that the approach highlighted by her research has better results than 'other ways of learning to read with the primary emphasis on sounds, letters or sight words' (12).

Additional key figures who developed theories of reading and writing

Edmund Burke Huey (1870-1913)

Although we think of whole language approaches as being very much part of late twentieth century innovation, Huey had published a book in 1908 entitled *The Psychology and Pedagogy of Reading*. Huey was born in Pennsylvania in 1870 and died at a tragically young age. He advocated approaches to reading which could easily have been written in the last five or ten years. In the foreword (written in the 1970s) to the book there is a reminder that Huey raised questions to which the science of that time could not provide answers. The writer suggests that more recent developments in psychology, linguistics and psycholinguistics might have allowed him to answer things which troubled him.

Huey suggests that:

- whenever possible learning to read should occur in the home
- learning to read should not become a chore or a 'fetish'
- the initial focus should be on whole sentences rather than individual sounds or words
- literature should be enjoyed from the earliest days
- phonics teaching should be delayed (but not neglected).

His work is visionary, and when republished in the late 1960s was taken up by many reading reformers. They had reached similar conclusions in a vastly different era and with different scientific tools at their disposal. The 1960s and 70s saw a firm emphasis on real books or good literature, home reading with the strong involvement of parents and a shift away from beginning with phonics methods.

Another interesting area of discussion in Huey's work concerns his views on the early days of schooling. His words echo the theories of Dewey *(How*

Children Learn pages 21–22) and Steiner (How Children Learn pages 26–28) when he writes (21):

> 'whether at school or at home, the young child is to be occupied mainly with quite other matters than formal exercises in learning to read, until his eighth year at least... the natural bases of a school course for this early period, dominated as it should be by oral rather than by printed and written work, full of good literature... real acquaintanceship with outdoor nature..., well-directed muscular development in free play and in manual work, singing, illustrative drawing, picture writing, perhaps some conversational work in a foreign language, these and other activities suited to this stage of the child's development will make the school session wholesome delight instead of a burden, to child and teacher alike.'

It is not known how much influence Huey had during his lifetime, but his views chimed with those of people wanting to reform approaches to reading in the latter part of the twentieth century.

Frank Smith

Frank Smith is a psycholinguist who has made a tremendous impact on theories of reading during the 1980s. He was a reporter, editor, and novelist before beginning his formal research into language, thinking, and learning. Although born in England, he completed his PhD at Harvard University and has held professorships at universities in Canada and South Africa. His views were challenging and throughout the 1970s and 1980s caused many people to rethink their approach to literacy. He worked closely with Kenneth Goodman. His key message was 'learn to read by reading'.

Amongst the most famous of Smith's publications is an essay (13) entitled Twelve Easy Ways to Make Learning to Read Difficult. In the light of the current debate about reading in the early years it is particularly interesting to note that the first two rules are:

• Aim for early mastery of the rules of reading, and
• Ensure that phonic skills are learned and used.

Smith was very opposed to phonics approaches but we should be careful to differentiate between knowing sound/letter correspondences and using those in order to build up words (which as discussed later in this section is what synthetic phonics set out to teach). His objections were for two main reasons. Firstly, quoting research which showed that 166 rules would be needed to deal with the most frequent patterns in 6000 high frequency one- and two-syllable words, he claimed that phonics approaches would be too 'unreliable and cumbersome' (14). Secondly he underlined that sounding out (or building up) words is the last strategy used by competent readers.

In response to the question 'what is the best method of teaching reading?' Smith wrote (15):

I will not give testimonials for methods ... For a start, most 'methods' are subject to wide ranges of interpretation; what one teacher claims to be doing in the name of a particular method may be nothing like what other adherents of the same label subscribe to. And then, even the most sensible of devices and techniques is subject to misuse in the hands of certain teachers. ... But, most important, I do not think methods help children accomplish anything they might usefully want to learn; teachers must do that. Teachers who need to be told the best method would probably not be capable of succeeding with it, even if it existed.... All that children need is competent people to help them make sense of and make use of written language

Kenneth and Yetta Goodman
A husband and wife team who still live and work in Arizona, they are widely viewed as being responsible for developing 'whole language' approaches to reading and writing. *What's Whole in Whole Language?* is just one example of the hundreds of books written by them.

Margaret Meek
Margaret Meek is still a professor at the Institute of Education in London. In the 1980s she was particularly noted for her work on reading with 'real' books. Her most well-known books are probably *On Being Literate*, a highly readable book aimed at parents on how children learn to read. Her encyclopaedic knowledge of children's books led her to write about the ways in which good literature supports children's learning. One such example was entitled *How Texts Teach What Children Learn*.

Sylvia Ashton-Warner
Spinster – a book written in 1958 – is an account of Sylvia Ashton-Warner teaching Maori children to read. Born in New Zealand, Ashton-Warner was an infant teacher all her life. Not until she retired did she take to writing. So gripping was this account of teaching reading that it was made into a film starring Shirley MacLaine. Her core method was to establish a personal Key

Vocabulary for each child, made up of words about which each individual was passionate. Her book is prefaced with a quote which says 'I want the one rapture of an inspiration' – and her teaching and her book are just that – inspirational.

Donald Graves

Donald Graves is an American. The focus of his work throughout the 1980s and on until the present day has been to develop the content of children's writing. He established the practice of writing conferences – teachers working with children to develop their stories and accounts. He currently offers an annual award for teachers developing the writing of primary aged children. His writing has consistently reflected the view that from their earliest marks on a page, children need to discover the power of writing. He writes that:

'it is important that the children we teach have a sense of what writing can do. It is just as important that we have a sense of what writing can do. The word I write on the page creates a picture of my own past.... Writing helps me to transcend myself in space and time.' (16)

The development of theories about writing

In 1975, Marie Clay published a book entitled *What did I write?* in which she encouraged teachers (and parents) to analyse children's unaided early attempts at writing. But it was in the 1980s that interest in the development of children's writing really grew. Two publications *Gnys at wrk* and *Literacy before schooling* were extremely influential.

Gnys at wrk (meaning Genius at Work) is a study of the author's son's writing development. She first noticed the strategies he was using when, unable to attract her attention because she was engrossed in some writing, he placed in front of her a sign which read R U DF (are you deaf?) She subsequently documented the development of his unaided writing.

Literacy before schooling describes a research project undertaken in South America in which the knowledge of writing in groups of young children is explored. The authors identified distinct characteristics in children's unaided writing. One such characteristic concerns their use of upper and lower case letters. When working unaided, children often prefer to use upper case letters and this may be due to motor control. The lines of upper case letters may be easier to reproduce than the characteristic curves of lower case letters. The author focused on children's drive to communicate, suggesting that for children in the early stages of learning to write it is harder to differentiate small b, d, p, f, g, etc than the relevant capital letters, as is the case with o, a, e or even u. From these and other similar studies, researchers identified stages in understanding of writing. What is now often termed 'have-a-go' writing or invented spelling stems directly from the theories which emerged as a result of these studies.

An American writer, L. Calkins (17), has suggested that the development of writing in young children, although drawing on a mixture of their experiences and what they have been taught, does not actually include clear developmental stages. She writes that:

'it is important to remember that what children do as writers depends on their backgrounds as writers. This is why ... sequence charts on writing are inadequate and perhaps harmful. Furthermore, even within any one writer, development does not consist of forward-moving progress. One day the writing is good, one day it is lousy, and often what seem at first to be regressions turn out to be the moments of imbalance through which new levels are reached'.

Twenty-first century developments

The literacy strategy was introduced in 1999. Although not compulsory, it quickly became standard practice, even in reception classes where it seemed to many practitioners to be inappropriate. Ten years earlier when the National Curriculum was introduced it had been claimed that although the government was determining what would be taught, it would never dictate how it should be taught. The introduction of the literacy strategy changed that.

The four part lesson (concluding with a plenary session) came to be seen as good practice. The theoretical underpinning for the strategy was labelled as searchlights – phonics, grammar, context and whole words. Drawing on best practice and a wide range of research, a team of experts led by John Stannard had identified these 'searchlights' as tools that children used to help them to decipher text.

By 2005, the failure of the literacy strategy to increase reading standards among the most disadvantaged groups had caused some unrest. The government commissioned a review of research into phonics (18). It reported that there were no significant differences between different approaches. In the same year the Rose Review looking into the teaching of reading advised that all children should be taught 'first and fast' through an approach termed 'synthetic phonics'. The phonic approach promoted in the literacy strategy is termed 'analytic phonics' (see boxed text for a comparison of the two approaches). The Rose Review's recommendation was based heavily on a study carried out in Clackmannanshire in Scotland. The study has been widely criticised and the government's own commissioned report said it did not show that synthetic phonic approaches produced significant gains over other phonic approaches. For a full discussion of this debate see a report of TACTYC's 2006 conference entitled Reading Between the Lines (19). Studies of a wide range of research showed greatest gains occurred where children had the greatest awareness of language as a whole.

Both the Rose Review and research into language (see The development of theories about how children learn to talk) argue strongly that there must be an early focus on talking. Awareness of and competence in spoken language are key to developing effective literacy.

The phonics debate (20)

Analytic phonics	Synthetic phonics
Analytic phonics works in the opposite way by breaking words down into constituent sounds, and asking children to recognise phrases and sounds. A child learning to read 'catch' with synthetic phonics would read it with c-a-t-ch. In analytic phonics it would be cat-ch	Synthetic phonics teaches children to read based on the 44 sounds made by letters or small groups of letters (phonemes) which comprise English. Once the letters denoting these sounds (21 consonants, 5 vowels, and double-letter sounds such as ch, sh, th, oo, ee, etc.) can be recognised, the child is taught to blend them into words (eg. c-a-t, s-t-r-ee-t)
Involves analysis of whole words to detect phonetic or spelling patterns	Starts with mapping letters to sounds
Teaches the sounds of letters in the contexts of words – children learn to break words down rather than build them up	Builds words up from individual letters – sounds synthesised (or blended) to produce different words

Considers an 'onset' (initial letter or phoneme/sound) and then the rest of the word (rime)	Children learn phonemes (the smallest unit of sound) and the corresponding written symbols (or graphemes such as 'ow' and 'ough')
Particularly effective with words that cannot easily be worked out sound by sound	Particularly useful in words that are phonetically regular
Taught alongside whole language approaches - which research shows to be effective	Involves systematic whole class teaching plus group work
Efficient way to develop a large sight vocabulary for reading and spelling	Involves a multi-sensory approach, seeing the symbol, listening to the sound, saying the sound and accompanying this with an action
Criticisms: The approach is said to take too long to help children decode unknown text, can be confusing for children and relies too much on guesswork	Criticisms: This approach is said to be boring and meaningless. It is insufficiently individualized and although it teaches children to decode text relatively quickly it may get in the way of both comprehension and enjoyment. Some criticisms stem from the fact that the loudest advocates include many people who have a very strong commercial interest in synthetic phonic schemes
Benefits: This approach sits comfortably with traditional early years practice in that it focuses on what children know and are interested in. Rather than teaching (and using) letters and sounds in a pre-programmed order, it encourages children to use what is familiar and meaningful to them (such as the letters of their name)	Benefits: Advocates claim that the results in Clackmannanshire show enhanced results. Others claim that children learning English as a second language, learn to read faster

The development of theories about how children learn to read and write

Comment

The history of approaches to reading and writing is long and complicated and this section can do no more than give a flavour of the debate that has raged (as Huey's work (21) shows) over many years. Much of the conflict hinges on what reading is believed to be for, and what it actually is.

The introduction of free and compulsory education in 1870 set out to make large numbers of children, most of whom came from families where no-one else could read, literate. Expectations were not high and the methods developed focused on a small number of skills, which employers increasingly demanded.

Times have changed – not only are most people able to read, but children are completely bombarded by print. Moreover, we know much more about effective learning and teaching and about the social and emotional aspects of learning. Methods which might have been effective in 1870 may not be so today.

Literacy has many political aspects. The introduction of universal schooling was a political act and the demand for the wholesale introduction of synthetic phonics is a political act. It has wrongly been suggested that phonics have been neglected. This is far from the case – the debate is about those responsible for the teaching of young children having not merely the right, but the responsibility, to make decisions about how children should be taught.

Paradoxically, the drive to standardise the teaching of phonics for our youngest children comes alongside calls for personalised learning and teaching for older children.

References

(1)   Beard, R. (1987) Developing Reading 3 – 13 *Dunton Green Sevenoaks: Hodder and Stoughton*

(2)   Clark, M. (1976) Young Fluent Readers *London: Heinemann (page 74)*

(3)   Beard 1987 (page 74), citing Petherick's Progressive Phonic Primer

(4)   Schonell, F. (1962) (4th ed) (first published 1945) The Psychology and Teaching of Reading *London: Oliver and Boyd (page 12)*

(5)   example taken from http://news.bbc.co.uk/1/hi/uk/1523708.stm

(6)   McNally, J. and Murray, W. (1968) Key Words to Literacy *London: Schoolmaster Publishing Co.*

(7)   Beard, R. (1987) Developing Reading 3 – 13 *Sevenoaks: Hodder and Stoughton, based on pages 81-82 citing Goodacre 1971*

(8)   Moon, C. (2006) Individualised Reading. *http://www.schooltrain. info/english/reading/cliff_moon.htm*

(9)   Holdaway, D. (1979) The Foundations of literacy *London: Ashton Scholastic (page 12)*

(10)   *NLS: Review of research and other related evidence http:// www.standards.dfes.gov.uk/primary/publications/literacy/ 63541/651161/919183*

(11)   Clay, M. (1982) Observing Young Readers: selected papers *Portsmouth, New Hampshire: Heinemann (page 174)*

(12)   Clay, M. (1982) Observing Young Readers: selected papers *Portsmouth, New Hampshire: Heinemann (page 29)*

(13)   Twelve Easy Ways to Make Learning to Read Difficult *in Smith (1983)*

(14)   Smith, F. (1983) Essays into Literacy *London: Heinemann*

(15)   Smith, F. (1983) Essays into Literacy *London: Heinemann (page 142)*

(16)   Graves, D. (1991) Build a Literate Classroom *London: Heinemann*

(17)   Calkins, L. (1986) The art of teaching writing *Portsmouth, New Hampshire: Heinemann (page 33)*

(18)   *Torgerson, Brooks and Hall (2005) A systematic review of research on the use of phonics in the teaching of reading and spelling DfES*

(19)   *Wyse, D. (2006) Rose Tinted Spectacles. Synthetic Phonics, Research Evidence and the Teaching of Reading. www.tactyc.org. uk/pdfs/2006conf_wyse.pdf*

(20)   *Blair, A, Halpin, T. (2005) Synthetic phonics replaces unsound literacy strategy. http://www.timesonline.co.uk/tol/news/politics/ article744794.ece and Edgington, M. (2006) 'Why the fuss about phonics?' In Featherstone, S. (ed) L is for sheep – getting ready for phonics Lutterworth: Featherstone Education Ltd.*

(21)   Huey, E. B. (1968) The Psychology and Pedagogy of Reading *Cambridge, Mass.: MIT (first published in 1908 by The Macmillan Company) (pages 336–337)*

Where to find out more

Literacy trust website for research, news and general updates on literacy www.literacytrust.org.uk

Read about Marie Clay and Reading Recovery http://readingrecovery.org

For more information on Don Holdaway and shared reading see http://www.standards.dfes.gov.uk/primary/publications/ literacy/63541/651161/919183

Meyer, R. (2002) Phonics Exposed – understanding and resisting systematic direct intense phonics instruction London: Lawrence Erlbaum Associates

The development of theories about intelligence

INTRODUCTION

Ideas about the nature of intelligence, its characteristics and whether it is inherited and fixed or subject to change, were developed throughout the twentieth century. Interest in intelligence began with the work of Darwin in the middle of the nineteenth century and the theories that emerged were not to be seriously challenged until the publication of Howard Gardner's book Frames of Mind in 1983.

KEY DATES

1822-1911
Francis Galton

1857-1911
Alfred Binet

1859
Origin of the Species
published by Charles Darwin

1863-1945
Charles Spearman

1869
Hereditary Genius
published by Galton

1871-1938
Wilhelm (often known as
William) Stern

Key figures in the development of theories of intelligence

Francis Galton (1822-1911)

The work of Charles Darwin on evolution led to widespread interest among scientists of the day about the nature of intellect. Darwin's cousin, Francis Galton, followed up this interest by studying the lives of a range of eminent or successful people. Galton's conclusion was that intelligence was inherited and that, across the population, intelligence could be seen to follow a pattern of natural distribution. This is sometimes described as a bell curve and simply means that most of the population will have levels of intelligence around the average score, while small numbers of people will have either very high or very low intelligence scores. It is this theory of distribution that has given rise to the use of terms such as percentiles and standard deviations. These are used not only to describe intelligence but also, for example, to compare individual babies' weights to average weights.

Galton went on to develop this theory by gathering a large amount of data. This in turn led him to pioneer the use of mental tests which (in these early stages of thinking about intelligence) measured reaction times and fine sensory discrimination (1). He discovered the phenomenon, now termed 'regression to the mean'. This means that, for example, particularly tall, or short, or intelligent parents tend to have children whose characteristics are closer to average. Galton also favoured eugenics, which seeks to improve on human nature by selective breeding. He did not believe that everyone is born equal and wanted to improve on nature.

Alfred Binet (1857-1911)

Although born in Nice in Southern France, from the age of 15 Binet lived and worked in Paris. Originally studying law and medicine, he eventually took up natural sciences and psychology, which was at that time a new subject. Like Freud, Binet spent some time studying with Charcot, renowned for his work on hypnosis. Following the births of his two daughters in 1885 and 1887, Binet began to maintain a diary of observations of their behaviour and development. This was not unusual at this time – indeed there was what is sometimes known as The Child Study Movement (2). In 1877, Charles Darwin published his observations of his son Doddy. During the twentieth century this tradition was notably carried on by Jean Piaget (see How Children Learn page 37). What was particularly interesting about Binet's baby biographies (3) was the fact that he did not just observe but tried out some simple

The development of theories about intelligence

experiments. In the process of reflecting on and analysing what his children did, Binet appears to have developed ideas about intelligence and how to measure it. He also developed some work on the conservation of number which was an aspect of development later given prominence by Piaget. Perhaps we should not be surprised about this – although Binet himself did not work with Piaget, his colleague Simon (with whom he developed intelligence tests) did.

Although Galton had started to devise some measures of intelligence, Alfred Binet is generally credited with developing the first real intelligence tests (4). Binet believed that the tests being developed on sensory responses by Galton were too simple and that more complex tests were needed. He explored the more complex notions of 'comprehension, judgment, reasoning and invention' (5). Over time he added a number of practical tasks drawing on children's day-to-day knowledge. Binet had been approached in 1900 by the Parisian authorities and asked to devise a test which would determine whether or not children were sufficiently intelligent to benefit from school attendance.

In 1905 Binet, with his colleague Theodore Simon devised a series of such tests, geared to identifying children who would be unable to cope with mainstream schooling and would therefore need some form of remedial education. These were known as the Simon-Binet tests. The idea that children could be helped and that intelligence could be developed is not one which Galton had held – but it was central to the work of Binet. Binet argued that the scores arrived at through testing should not be seen as wholly accurate since the brain can reorganise or regenerate itself.

Binet himself was undoubtedly influenced by the earlier work of Itard (1775-1838) and Seguin (1812–1880), both of whom had worked with children labelled by many at that time as ineducable. Their work was also to have a great influence on Maria Montessori (see *How Children Learn* pages 29–31) when she worked with what were then known as 'retarded' children in Rome.

The tests which Binet and Simon devised were said to have three roots. Some of the tests relied on medical information – what they themselves referred to as 'the anatomical, physiological, and pathological signs of inferior intelligence'. Other tests were said to rely on pedagogy or what had been taught and learnt. The third group – which Binet regarded as the most important – focused on psychological aspects of behaviour such as reasoning.

KEY DATES

1874-1949
Edward Thorndike

1877-1956
Lewis Terman

1883-1971
Cyril Burt

1896-1981
David Wechsler

1897-1987
Joy Paul Guilford

1900
Binet asked to develop a measure for predicting success or failure at school

1912
Wilhelm Stern developed first measure of IQ

1921
Lewis Terman introduced first longitudinal study of giftedness

1983
Frames of Mind published by Howard Gardner

The development of theories about intelligence

Sample test items from Binet and Simon's Measuring Scale of intelligence 1911(6)

This table sets out some of the tests, graded according to age, devised by Alfred Binet and his colleague Theodore Simon:

Four years	able to name a key, knife and penny, repeat three figures and compare the length of two lines
Six years	able to distinguish between morning and evening; copy a diamond shape and count thirteen pennies
Eight years	able to compare two objects from memory; count from twenty to zero and repeat a string of five digits

Charles Spearman (1863-1945)

Spearman began his career in the army, but in 1897 after fifteen years he went to Germany to study experimental psychology with one of the pioneering figures in psychology, Wilhelm Wundt. By the time he received his degree he had already published a seminal paper on the factor analysis of intelligence (1904). Spearman subsequently moved to London University and in 1928 became Professor of Psychology when a separate Department of Psychology was created. He was strongly influenced by the work of Francis Galton and like him was particulary interested in the correlation between intelligence and other characterisitcs of people.

Wilhelm Stern (1871-1938)

In 1912, Stern invented the term intelligence quotient, nowadays usually referred to simply as IQ. It is a figure which is arrived at by calculating a person's mental age or intelligence test score and dividing it by their actual (or chronological) age. This number is then multiplied by 100.

A child scoring at 3 years 6 months on an intelligence test at the age of 3 years 9 months would be said to have an IQ of 93. An average score (where the test score or mental age is the same as the real age) would be 100. In this case the child is scoring slightly below their chronological age.
$3.5 \div 3.75 \times 100 = 93.33$

A five year old child scoring at the level of a seven year old would be said to have an IQ of 140, which would be considered to be the mark of a gifted child.
$7 \div 5 \times 100 = 140$

Edward Thorndike (1874-1949)

The work of the American, Edward Thorndike, as a behavioural psychologist has been very briefly outlined in *How Children Learn* (page 42). His interest in problem-solving was linked to an interest in the measurement of intelligence. In 1927 he published a book entitled *The Measurement of Intelligence*. In his view most intelligence tests were only focused on abstract intelligence. He believed that both mechanical intelligence (the ability to understand how the physical world works) and social intelligence (the ability to deal with other people successfully) were equally important. In addition he argued that in considering abstract intelligence, tests should take account of four dimensions – namely the difficulty and variety of tasks offered as well as their scope or area and the speed with which they were completed. Thorndike was also interested in what he termed connectionism. Referring to the neural connections developed in the brain, he suggested that higher levels of intelligence made it possible for more bonds to be formed more easily. Thus he suggested those of lower ability would have greater difficulty in making connections. He, like Galton working half a century before him, believed that this ability was largely inherited – although he did think that the content of the thinking and making connections depended on experience. This view has many important echoes in work on the brain in the twenty-first century, particularly amongst those studying creativity (see the chapter on the development of theories about creativity).

Lewis Terman (1877-1956)

Terman's name is widely associated with a range of intelligence tests. Building on Stern's ideas about the measurement of IQ, he released in 1916 the 'Stanford Revision of the Binet-Simon Scale' or the 'Stanford-Binet' for short, drawing the name from the university at which he was then employed. During the course of the First World War, Terman developed widespread testing on American soldiers in an effort to place men in the roles best suited to their IQ.

In the early 1920s, an influential journalist, Walter Lippmann, criticised Terman's use of IQ testing, which seemed to indicate that the average mental age of American adults was 14 years. In 1922, Terman is said to have suggested that nothing is of more importance than IQ. Lippmann responded quickly with a series of critical essays. He was among the first to draw attention to the possible cultural bias of IQ tests and to the social inequalities which they underlined.

In 1927 he further revised the Stanford-Binet tests, developing a version which became known as the Terman and Merrill tests. These tests took their name from the co-director of the project, Maude Merrill.

Cyril Burt (1883-1971)

Burt was strongly influenced by Galton's theory of intelligence. He, like Galton, firmly believed that intelligence is inherited. In fact, he stated that 80% of intelligence is inherited and not therefore subject to change (7). It is sometimes claimed that it was Burt who developed the first written IQ tests. His tests were developed for schoolchildren, unlike Terman's initial work which focused on developing tests for categorising soldiers. Burt's tests were designed to be used by classroom teachers in order to help them to identify both the children who, it was deemed, would not benefit from ordinary schooling and those who were gifted. He contributed to the writing of the 1944 Education Act which introduced the 11+ exam, which relied heavily on intelligence testing.

Although Burt was for a long time highly influential and was regarded as having considerable skills in academic, practical and political fields of work, his work has now been discredited. His most famous work was based on the study of a large number of identical twins separated at birth and reared in contrasting situations. It was claimed that this study proved that intelligence was inherited and not due to upbringing. The study was accepted and influenced views of intelligence for some considerable time.

Five years after his death, however, it was discovered that the data from this work had been falsified. He had not only made up data to support his own views, but had invented researchers. This was a shocking discovery that underlines many of the central debates around intelligence. For those, like Burt, who believe that intelligence is mainly inherited, it is perhaps important to ensure that money and time are not wasted on trying to develop children in ways which will not change their nature. Many others now believe of course that intelligence tests do not measure inherited factors, but reflect causal factors such as poverty, social class or ethnicity. For those who believe that intelligence is nurtured, it is vitally important for the well-being of individuals and nations to ensure that opportunities are broadened and high quality education safeguarded for all.

Florence Goodenough (1886-1959)

Goodenough studied with Terman. She worked with children until she became a professor in the 1940s. She devised the Goodenough Draw-a-Man test (now generally known as the draw-a-person test). The test is very simple, children simply being asked to draw a person. Their drawing is then given a score which is based on the number of features they have included. Despite some criticisms – largely based on whether or not the tests actually measure intelligence – the test remains very popular. In addition to its use with children, the test (with various scoring schemes) is widely used in medical circles to test, for example, adult stroke patients or those with a range of psychological disturbances. It is simple to administer but is probably only useful as part of a battery of tests.

David Wechsler (1896-1981)

Wechsler devised intelligence tests which today remain amongst the most widely used. He defined intelligence as 'the global capacity to act purposefully, to think rationally and to deal effectively with one's environment' (8). In 1939 he developed an intelligence test for adults, which was followed ten years later by a test for children. The preschool and primary test (known as WPPSI) was originally developed in 1967. It is regularly revised to take account of the Flynn effect (see box). The Wechsler Preschool and Primary Scale of Intelligence (9) uses the following tests:

1. Block Design – the child uses one or two-colour blocks to re-create a given design within a specified time limit.
2. Information – the child responds to a question by choosing a picture from four response options and, in order to test verbal ability, answers questions which address a broad range of general knowledge topics.
3. Matrix Reasoning – the child looks at an incomplete grid or matrix and selects the missing portion from four or five possible solutions.
4. Vocabulary – the child names pictures set out in order of difficulty and gives definitions for words that the tester reads aloud.
5. Picture Concepts – the child is presented with two or three rows of pictures and chooses one picture from each row to form a group with a common characteristic.
6. Symbol Search – the child scans a search group and indicates whether a target symbol matches any of the symbols in the search group.
7. Word Reasoning – the child is asked to identify the common concept being described in a series of increasingly specific clues.
8. Coding – the child copies symbols that are paired with simple geometric shapes. Using a key, the child draws each symbol in its corresponding shape.
9. Comprehension – the child answers questions based on his or her understanding of general principles and social situations.

10. Picture Completion - the child views a picture and then points to or names the important missing part.
11. Similarities - the child is read an incomplete sentence containing two concepts that share a common characteristic. The child is asked to complete the sentence by providing a response that reflects the shared characteristic.
12. Receptive Vocabulary - the child looks at a group of four pictures and points to the one the examiner names aloud.
13. Object Assembly - the child is presented with the pieces of a puzzle in a standard arrangement and fits the pieces together to form a meaningful whole within 90 seconds.
14. Picture Naming - the child names pictures which are displayed in a stimulus book.

The Flynn Effect (10)

It has been noted over many years since intelligence testing began that test scores have been rising. This would suggest either that people are becoming more intelligent or that what is being measured is not actually intelligence, but abstract problem-solving skills. These effects are seen particularly strongly in the lowest achieving groups in society, but overall it is suggested that, taking the population as a whole, the average IQ has been gaining about 3 points every ten years.

There have been several suggested reasons for this which may include:

- Improved nutrition leading to greater intelligence
- Smaller families, with the younger children of large families often being seen as having lower levels of intelligence
- Better access to education with perhaps the possibility that people have become more used to tests and testing
- Earlier intervention through projects such as Sure Start or High/Scope (see *How Children Learn*, page 56)
- Increased complexity of the environment (including television, computer technology etc.) means that the human brain is becoming more flexible and adaptable.

Of course no one knows for sure what the real cause is – or perhaps it is a combination of these elements.

Joy Paul Guilford (1897-1987)

In 1904, Spearman suggested a two-factor model of intelligence, namely general intelligence which is involved in all tasks, and specific individual abilities that make a person more skilled at one task than another.

In 1967 Guilford refuted this idea as being too simple to explain human intelligence. Guilford offered a cube as a model for his view of intelligence. This provides 120 elements which make up the intellect. The dimensions of the cube (length, breadth and height) are described as operations (or general intellectual processes); content (or broad areas of information) and product (the result of applying particular operations to specific content).

Guilford's cube as a model for intelligence

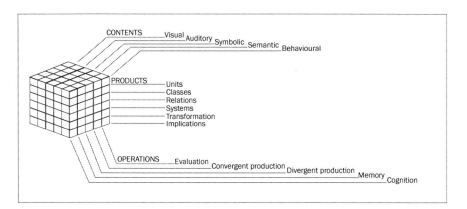

Aspects of intelligence proposed by Guilford (11)

operations	content	product
cognition (understanding, discovering etc.)	auditory	unit (a single item of information)
memory	symbolic (including verbal thinking and communication)	class (a set of items that share some characteristics or attributes)
divergent thinking (generating multiple solutions to problems)	semantic (information organized as symbols or signs that have no meaning by themselves, eg. numbers and letters of the alphabet)	relation (a connection between items)

convergent thinking (identifying a single solution to a problem)	behaviour	system (an organization of items or networks with interacting parts)
evaluation (judging whether an answer is accurate, consistent or valid)	visual	transformation (changing an item's attributes, eg. reversing order of letters in a word)
		implication (expectation or prediction)

Howard Gardner (born 1943)

Howard Gardner (see *How Children Learn* pages 63–66) was later to support Guilford's rejection of Spearman's idea of general intelligence. He, however, favoured not two, but six or eight, intelligences. As described in *How Children Learn*, Gardner set out to discredit the notion of intelligence as something inherited or fixed or indeed as something which could be measured. He reminds us that intelligence tests and the notion of IQ remained popular over many decades, because they provided an easy method for schools, hospitals and employment agencies to justify decisions about grading and sorting people. The early criticisms made by Lippmann, querying the reliability of scoring intelligence, are echoed by Gardner. He highlights (12) the way in which intelligence test scores tend to indicate that those with higher socio-economic standing achieve higher scores, and discusses the way in which traditional tests ignore practical intelligence or the increasing use of symbol systems. He further suggests (13) that:

'one reason I have moved away from attempting to create such measures is that they may lead to new forms of labelling and stigmatization... intelligences should be mobilized to help people learn important content and not used as a way of categorizing them... I do not want to inspire the creation of a new set of "losers"'.

The influence of developing theories about intelligence

One of the things which can be learnt from Burt's deception about the nature of intelligence is that the influence these developing theories of intelligence have had has often been shaped by external factors. Nature v nurture arguments are central to thinking about intelligence. While some people believe that intelligence is fixed, reliant wholly on our genes, others believe that upbringing or nurturing have a strong effect on intelligence. The answer is likely to be somewhere between these two extreme points of view. The relationship between genetic influence on learning and development and the impact of the environment in which children are brought up has sometimes been described as an intricate dance (14).

The nature argument about intelligence has often been used by societies which rely on one group of people being less important than others. In places where slavery is practised for example, the political and social situation is often justified by arguments about slaves being of less intelligence and therefore of less worth than the dominant group.

At one level, therefore, it could be said that the theories of intelligence themselves are influenced by other factors. Burt's data went unchallenged for many years because the view of intelligence which his studies confirmed was one held by most people.

Margaret McMillan (see *How Children Learn* pages 23–25) was a theorist and practitioner who firmly held the nurture side of the argument. Her experiences in poor parts of London showed her that the intelligence tests, which were gaining in popularity at the time as a way of classifying or categorising children, categorised many such children as subnormal. She recognized at an early stage that 'the stimulating environment of the nursery school enabled many to overcome the inhibiting effects of early deprivation' (15). It is something akin to this belief which has motivated politicians in the twenty-first century to fund Sure Start – a belief that breaking the cycle of deprivation supports improvements in the learning and development of young children.

Putting the theories into practice

Like many test scores and targets, intelligence tests are very attractive to administrators and policy makers because they allow something which is very difficult to categorise or pigeon-hole (namely people) to be grouped. Tests of this sort (often referred to as psychometric tests) are used in the assessment of children with special educational needs and in areas where 11+ testing still occurs. Gardner's point about labelling and stigmatization (see above) is an important one – especially for early years practitioners. Numbers attached to something as fluid and open to misrepresentation as IQ scores carry some risks – and those risks are that we limit children's opportunities. All too often the correlation which may be found between social class and test scores can mean that those who are most disadvantaged in social terms are further limited by low expectations and limited experiences.

One important factor which has had some impact on practice is the growing recognition that the brain is highly flexible and that it is therefore unlikely that intelligence is a fixed entity. This fits in with programmes such as Sure Start which have been set up in an effort to change the social conditions which affect achievement in school.

Comment

It has been pointed out that people who devise intelligence tests value most the things that they themselves are good at. Intelligence tests therefore tend to focus on things which enabled them to succeed at school (16). It is important to remember that what counts as intelligence varies markedly between societies and cultures. The table below sets out some of the differences in cultural views of intelligence (16).

Cultural group	Words and phrases associated with intelligence
Chinese students	memory for facts
Australian students	memory seen as trivial in relation to intelligence
Ugandan villagers	slow, careful, active, knowing how to and acting in socially appropriate ways
Ugandan teachers (and other westernized groups)	speed
middle-class groups in USA	abstract thinking; technical ability (but not social and emotional intelligence)
Some African groups' view of children's intelligence	social responsibility; cooperativeness and obedience
Malay students	social and cognitive attributes
Ifaluk of western Pacific	knowledge and performance of good social behaviour

The development of theories about intelligence

As Gardner's theory has reminded us, intelligence is not a fixed aspect of human behaviour. Children, like everyone else, act intelligently in some situations and not in others. One of the major problems with intelligence testing has been a failure to acknowledge that simply being in a test situation makes it more difficult for many children to demonstrate their real knowledge and understanding.

Theories about intelligence remain incomplete. The American Psychological Association set up a task force in the late 1990s and outlined areas which need further research (16). These include:

- The impact of genes on intelligence is not fully known
- Aspects of environment which affect intelligence are not yet fully known
- The relationship between nutrition and intelligence is not fully known
- Neither the Flynn effect nor the differences in intelligence test scores between groups have been fully explained
- Insufficient is known about aspects of human behaviour (such as creativity, wisdom or social sensitivity) which are not readily measured by intelligence tests.

References

(1)   Gardner, H. et al (1996) Intelligence: multiple perspectives *London: Harcourt Brace College Publishers*

(2)   Bartholomew, L. & Bruce, T. (1993) Getting to Know You *London: Hodder and Stoughton*

(3)   Bergin, D. & Cizek, G. (2001) 'Alfred Binet' In Palmer, J. (ed) Fifty Major Thinkers on Education *London: Routledge*

(4)   Gardner, H. (1999) Intelligence Reframed *New York: Basic Books*

(5)   Gardner, H. et al (1996) Intelligence: multiple perspectives *London: Harcourt Brace College Publishers (page 47 citing Binet and Simon 1916)*

(6)   Gardner, H. et al (1996) Intelligence: multiple perspectives *London: Harcourt Brace College Publishers (page 49)*

(7)   Ridgway, J. (2001) 'Cyril Lodovic Burt' In Palmer, J. (ed) Fifty Major Thinkers on Education *London: Routledge*

(8)   Kaplan, R. and Saccuzzo, D. (2004) Psychological testing: principles, applications and issues. *(6th ed) Wadsworth (page 256)*

(9)   based on *http://en.wikipedia.org/wiki/Wechsler_Preschool_ and_Primary_Scale_of_Intelligence*

(10)   Neisser, U. (1997) 'Rising Scores on Intelligence Tests'. American

Scientist *85: 440-447*

(11) Guilford, J.P. *Stricture of Intellect. http://tip.psychology.org/ guilford.html*

(12) Gardner, H. (1999) Intelligence Reframed *New York: Basic Books*

(13) Gardner, H. (2006) *Multiple Intelligences: new horizons New York: Basic Books (page 70)*

(14) Karmiloff-Smith, A. (2001) 'Why babies' brains are not Swiss army knives' In Rose, H. and Rose, S. (eds) *Alas Poor Darwin: arguments against evolutionary psychology London: Vintage*

(15) Whitbread, N. (1975) The Evolution of the Nursery-Infant School *London: Routledge and Kegan Paul*

(16) Deary, I. (2001) Intelligence: a very short introduction *Oxford: Oxford University Press (page 121 gives details of the findings of the American Psychological Association)*

Where to find out more

Gardner, H. et al (1996) Intelligence: multiple perspectives *London: Harcourt Brace College Publishers*

Neisser, U. et al (1996) Intelligence: knowns and unknowns. *American Psychologist 51: 77-101*

Palmer, J. (ed) (2001) Fifty Major Thinkers on Education *London: Routledge*

The development of theories about creativity

Overview of the development of thinking about creativity

Creativity is an elusive quality, but described by some writers (1) as the thing that makes us human.

Historical perspectives

Creativity itself is believed to have emerged in humans 40,000 or 50,000 years ago in a period of history known as the human revolution or the creative explosion (2). Its emergence was marked by a growing ability in humans to think in the abstract and therefore to plan as a group, to create new ideas and objects and to use symbols, including signs, images and increasingly more sophisticated language.

It has been suggested (3) that scientific thinking about creativity began in the 1950s. It is difficult to determine exactly when such interest started because the use of the term creativity was not widespread. Many researchers had been looking at aspects of creative thinking – such as thinking, problem-solving and imagination. However, this date is widely accepted as marking the beginning of widespread interest because it was in 1950 that Guilford (see the chapter on the development of theories about intelligence) gave a talk to the American Psychological Association on the subject of creativity.

It has been further suggested (4) that the Second World War led to the first wave of interest in creativity as both sides of the conflict tried to gain the upper hand by developing ever more lethal weapons. Some of the creative gains that emerged from that period were to have much wider applications – for example, nylon fabrics were developed in order to develop parachutes which did not require the expensive and scarce silk which had been used up to that time.

At the end of the Second World War, it became obvious that many of the creative ideas developed, such as the atomic bomb, were 'threatening the well-being of the planet' (4). By the end of the twentieth century it had become increasingly apparent that life, as we know it, was under threat from a great many of our own creative ideas. This means that 'creativity is needed more than ever before. New adaptations are necessary. The matter is urgent' (4). So, paradoxically, we are constantly seeking new ideas to deal with the effects of our earlier good ideas. It has also meant that governments want to develop young minds that have high creative potential through the education system with, for example, a focus on children regarded as 'gifted and talented'.

Creativity is greatly prized in humans. Because we make frequent and significant changes to our environment, our brains have to be flexible and creative. While most animals can rely on reflex action, humans must constantly find new solutions to match our changing lives.

KEY DATES

c.45,000 BC
The beginning of the human revolution or creative explosion

1897-1987
Joy Paul Guilford

1905-1983
Arthur Koestler

1915-2003
Ellis Paul Torrance

1933
Birth of Edward de Bono

1934
Birth of Mihaly Csikszentmihalyi

1939
First known use of the term brainstorming

1943
Birth of Howard Gardner

The development of theories about creativity

KEY DATES

1950
Guilford talks to American Psychological Association about creativity

1999
Publication of All our Futures

2003
Publication of Excellence and Enjoyment

There has also been interest in Britain, for example, in developing creativity more widely. When the government document *Excellence and Enjoyment* was published in 2003, the minister responsible talked about the start of a new revolution. Following the Industrial Revolution of the nineteenth century and the Technological Revolution of the twentieth century, the twenty-first century was to be described as the Creative Revolution. (In the light of archaeological findings, the minister might be judged as being 40,000 years behind the times.) Similarly, in China attempts are currently being made to change the curriculum in order to help children to be more creative.

Psychological perspectives

The work of Freud (see *How Children Learn* pages 17-20) has long been associated with creativity. From the psychoanalytical perspective which his theories offer, creativity represents an attempt to steer their sexual energy into what he saw as secondary pursuits such as drawing, writing and problem-solving. Freud also drew attention to the link between children's play, daydreaming and creativity. This view is echoed by many writers who emphasise the value of becoming child-like (or perhaps playful and curious) in the pursuit of creativity. Freud himself wrote (5):

> *'Might we not say that every child at play behaves like a creative writer, in that he creates a world of his own, or, rather, rearranges the things of his world in new way which pleases him?... The creative writer does the same as the child at play. He creates a world of phantasy which he takes very seriously – that is, which he invests with large amounts of emotion – while separating it sharply from reality.'*

The behaviourist perspective (based on the work of Skinner and others described in *How Children Learn* pages 42–43) emphasises the idea that creative people will have had their creativity positively rewarded or reinforced and therefore want to spend more time in their chosen pursuit. More recent studies both lend support to and challenge this view. It is clear from studies of experts in a number of fields (6) that people become expert (and thus more likely to be able to work creatively) after 10,000 hours of practice or engagement in their field. This view has been made memorable by the words of a journalist that 'even Mozart had to put in the hours' (7).

It is also likely that people will spend longer doing things that they feel they are good at, and this would seem to include feeling good at something because other people tell you how good you are. This view, however, is strongly challenged by research which shows that 'creative solutions to problems occur more often when individuals engage in an activity for its sheer pleasure than when they do so for possible external rewards' (8). The importance of intrinsic motivation has been shown in many studies of young children – when, for example, children given small rewards for drawing pictures stop drawing unless they are rewarded.

What do we mean by creativity?

'Creativity is a state of mind in which all of our intelligences are working together. It involves seeing, thinking and innovating. Although it is found in the creative arts, creativity can be found in any subject at school or in any aspect of life....' (Lucas, 2001, 38)

There are probably as many ideas about what creativity is as there are people who write about it. We might focus on the characteristics of creative people; the people who are creative or the ways in which creativity appears to be nurtured.

One thing is certain; creativity is not limited to the creative arts. Einstein was undoubtedly a creative mathematical and scientific thinker. Gandhi (9) has been described as socially creative or gifted. He described himself as 'an average mind with less than an average ability. I admit that I am not sharp intellectually. But I don't mind. There is a limit to the development of the intellect but none to that of the heart.' Apparently from the age of about eight he was given opportunities to advise older members of his family on moral and ethical problems.

However, the creative arts do have a special role to play in creativity. This is because they allow ideas to be represented and symbolised (ideas which link closely to those of Jerome Bruner and to the work developed in Reggio Emilia; more information on both can be found in *How Children Learn*).

What are the characteristics of creativity?
- In 1939 Alex Osborne, an advertising executive, coined the term brainstorming. For Guilford writing in the 1950s, the core aspect was perhaps divergent thinking. It would appear then that for both of these writers, having lots of ideas was the key to having creative ideas.
- Writers in the 1980s (10) identified six key characteristics – identifying patterns; making connections; risk-taking; questioning; seeing opportunities and seeing things in a new way. The ability to identify patterns and to make connections are supported by brain research.

Humans are born pattern seekers. From the moment of birth babies seek out patterns which are like human faces. Throughout life we try to form and identify patterns in order to be able to make sense of the world and to predict. Making connections is what the brain does all the time. Finding something new, the brain looks for something similar to which it can link. The link creates an electrical connection which helps us to link up to other similar people, events or experiences. If the brain is unable to find or create a connection it will not perceive or learn from the new experience. The other of these six characteristics on which comment should be made is that of risk-taking. A number of recent publications remind parents and practitioners that we are hindering learning and creativity by making children's environments too safe.

- *All our futures*, which was published in 1999, identifies just four aspects involved in creativity. Imagination; purposeful activity; originality and critical awareness are seen as its vital components. Purposeful activity does not necessarily imply a pre-determined outcome. Just as young children often take some chance sound, image or event as their starting point, so it is with creative adults (11). Children may be purposeful in their decision to draw, may even decide they are going to draw mummy. Then on beginning to draw a line they are reminded of a dog and they work on that idea. This is not confined to children. In Pech Merle in France there is a very famous cave painting of a spotted horse which was painted around 25,000 years ago. The muzzle of the horse is not painted, but based around the shape of the rock itself. The artist clearly saw the shape of the stone and made the connection that it looked like a horse.
- Imagination is consistently seen as an important element in creativity. This has been referred to as possibility thinking (12) or 'the concept of what might be – being able to move in perception from the concrete given, or "what is" to "what was, what could have been, what one can try for, what might happen" and ultimately, to the purest realms of fantasy – is a touchstone of that miracle of human experience, the imagination'.

What counts as original?

'Society continues to be transformed by the advent of new technologies, such as the wheel, television, the computer, and atomic energy. They arise from the efforts of creative individuals, from the power of new ideas. ...First, it must be recognized that such creativity builds on the technologies already available within existing institutions. A creative idea is in some sense a reformulation of existing ideas; there is nothing completely new under the

sun. Something completely new would not even be recognized. Creative approaches are ideas that forge a new connection between ideas and tools that are already familiar. Creativity lies in the capacity to see more sharply and with greater insight that which one already knows or that which is buried at the margins of one's awareness.... Second, individual creativity occurs in the context of a community of thinkers... where more than one person is working on the solution of a particular problem or within the particular genre of expression.' (Rogoff 1990, page 198)

Being original involves expressing ideas and feelings in new ways. This may seem difficult for children to achieve since their experience and skills are necessarily limited. Ken Robinson (who chaired the group which wrote All Our Futures) describes originality in three ways – as personal (something that is new for me), social (something that is new within my community) and finally as historic (something which has not been previously thought of or developed). Tina Bruce (13) offers some similar categories which she calls everyday creators, specialist creators and world-shattering creators.

'Big C' or 'little c' creativity?

Steven Pinker (as the boxed quote on the following page shows) believes that the creativity shown by geniuses is essentially the same as the creativity shown by you and me. However, Howard Gardner takes a rather different point of view. He has written extensively of 'Big C' and 'little c' creativity since he believes (as the quote from one of his books below shows) that while we all have a measure of creativity, creative geniuses have qualities which are theirs alone.

For those of us who work with young children, such a distinction is one we cannot afford to make. Whether we believe that especially creative individuals are made or nurtured – born extra creative or made extra creative by their experiences and upbringing – we have a responsibility to act as though all will be especially creative. Then perhaps they will be?

All of us are creative. Every time we stick a handy object under the leg of a wobbly table or think of a new way to bribe a child into his pajamas (sic), we have used our faculties to create a novel outcome. But creative geniuses are distinguished not just by their extraordinary works but by their extraordinary way of working; they are not supposed to think like you and me... But they are not freaks with minds utterly unlike ours or unlike anything we can imagine evolving in a species that has always lived by its wits. The genius creates good ideas; that is what our ... minds are for. Pinker, S. (1998) How the Mind Works London: The Penguin Press (pages 360-362)

The development of theories about creativity

Recent studies have yielded two major findings. On the one hand, creative individuals do not seem to have at their disposal mental operations that are theirs alone; they make use of the same cognitive processes others do, but they use them in a more efficient and flexible way and in the service of goals that are ambitious and often quite risky..... On the other hand, highly creative individuals seem to lead their lives differently than most others. They are fully engaged in and passionate about their work; they exhibit a need to do something new and a strong sense of their purpose and ultimate goals; they are extremely reflective about their activities, their use of time, and the quality of their products....
Gardner, H. (2006) Multiple Intelligences – new horizons New York: Basic Books (pages 177)

Exploding myths about creativity

Creativity is not a separate faculty that some people have and others do not.

Creativity is not something which only some families have. It is simply not true to say that only children born to musical families can be musically creative. It is not an innate talent given to the few. Nor is it true to say that you're either born creative or not and nothing more can be done about it. We're all born creative.

It is not true that only a genius can be creative.

Creativity is not just about the arts. It can be (and is) found in every field of human endeavour.

Creativity is not the same as performance. There are creative performances but if we only ever ask children to perform other people's songs, for example, they will be missing out on important creative opportunities. Performance allows creative plays, songs, music and so on to be shared with others.

Creative people are not doomed to be unhappy or temperamental.

Creativity is not all about revolution and chaos. It is, however, seeking out change and thus may feel threatening.

The curriculum is not too crowded to take on creativity. In fact, creativity is a way of approaching everything. Each of us is likely to be more creative in

---

some areas of expertise than others, but we can learn from each other. Everyone's playfulness and curiosity can support a creative ethos.

(based on Bruce 2004)

The links between creativity and intelligence

In the section of this book entitled The development of theories about intelligence, the way in which intelligence came to be seen as fixed and measurable has been described. By the middle of the twentieth century interest in creativity had developed and Guilford, who was particularly interested in psychometrics (or psychological testing), set about promoting the idea of testing to find out which individuals had creative potential. Decades later it has become apparent that:

- intelligence and creativity are not the same. Some people who are tested as highly creative may not show similar levels of intelligence and vice versa;
- creativity test scores are reliable – in that any individual is likely to get a similar score on each one of a battery of creativity tests;
- scores on a creativity test do not help to predict who is or is not creative in real-life situations. In short 'creativity tests have made little difference in the broader research and educational communities' (13).

'In the post-Sputnik era, when scientific ingenuity was suddenly at a premium, American educators became convinced of the importance of imaginativeness, inventiveness and creativity. They called for the devising of instruments that would assess creativity or creative potential (Guilford 1950, 1967). Regrettably (from my perspective), in their search for measures of creativity, they repeated most of the mistakes that had been made throughout the history of intelligence testing. That is, they tried to devise short-answer, timed measures of the abilities that [are] thought central to creativity – the capacity to come up with a variety of answers to a question (divergent thinking) or to issue as many unusual associations as possible to a stimulus (ideational fluency).

While the field of intelligence testing is filled with controversy, there is consensus that creativity tests have not fulfilled their potential... Rather than attempting to devise more and better creativity tests, researchers have instead begun to examine more closely what actually happens when individuals are engaged in problem-solving or problem-finding activities...' (14)

Educational approaches to creativity

'Except rhetorically the quest for creativity has not been a major goal of the American educational system. However, to the extent that fostering creative individuals is a desirable goal for an educational institution, it is important that this goal be pursued in a manner consistent with current analyses of creativity.'
Gardner, H. (2006) Multiple Intelligences – new horizons New York: Basic Books (page 177)

Until recent years it was not the goal of schools and education to develop creativity. When compulsory schooling was introduced in 1870, its aim was to produce people who would be able to read and write enough to enable them to fill out official forms and meet official requirements; who would be punctual and reliable and who would above all do as they were asked. Thinking for oneself was not what was required.

Being a free or innovative thinker is not always comfortable. Freud and Darwin were widely ridiculed in their lifetime. Bach and van Gogh were not well thought of until after their deaths and Einstein is said to have been a poor student and a late talker. Despite having created so much change, humans do not always like it and can perceive any challenge to things as they are as a threat. Even in a group of young children, the child who is always asking awkward questions or interpreting what they're asked to do differently than everyone else may be seen as a nuisance.

Now, however, there is a strong drive in many parts of the educational establishment to nurture creativity. Perhaps the most consistent work has been seen in Reggio Emilia (see *How Children Learn* pages 52-53). Bruner's work in Schools with Success, and Gardner's work with Project Zero (see *How Children Learn* pages 47-49 and 63-66 respectively) have also offered some interesting insights. In all these approaches there is a focus on the creative arts and an attempt to break away from over-reliance on traditional teacher-directed activity.

If fostering creativity in individuals is to be achieved in schools, it will be important to nurture the key characteristics of creativity:

• imagination
• identifying patterns
• making connections
• risk-taking

- questioning and curiosity
- the enthusiasm to see events, objects and opportunities with fresh eyes.

This means that in order to develop creativity children must have opportunities for:

- play and imagination
- social interaction and negotiation
- exploration and curiosity
- using a wide range of symbolic or representational media (see Loris Malaguzzi and early education in Reggio Emilia in *How Children Learn* pages 52–53)
- making connections, since we use what we know to link with what we don't know (15)
- experiencing the unexpected.

Adults need to ensure that children have:

- sufficient flexible use of time and space
- an environment in which they feel sufficiently safe to take risks
- opportunities to make decisions and experience the impact of those decisions
- encouragement to develop diligence and exuberance (or work and play, persistence and a sense of fun).

Some key figures in theories of creativity

Ken Robinson

Ken Robinson chaired the government committee (National Advisory Committee on Creativity and Culture in Education) which produced the report entitled *All our Futures*. The document focused on creativity in all sectors of education, but although it was published in 1999 it was relatively unknown until the publication of *Excellence and Enjoyment* in 2003. Robinson's work in creativity, education and training has earned him an international reputation. In 2000 he was voted Business Speaker of the Year. His book *Out of our minds: learning to be creative* (published in 2000) is highly readable. He is currently based at the University of Warwick.

Arthur Koestler (1905-1983)

Koestler was born in Hungary of a German speaking Jewish family. He later became a naturalised British subject. He spoke and wrote in a large number of languages and is described as a polymath – among his early achievements was an expedition to the North Pole.

Koestler's most celebrated, or perhaps best-known contribution to thinking about creativity, consists of what he calls the trinity of responses: aha; haha; and ah. The first (the 'aha') is perhaps most easily explained by thinking about Archimedes discovering that when he got into the bath, he displaced an amount of water equal in volume to the parts of his body which were under the water. His cry of 'Eureka' is described by Koestler as marking the creative act where something is not created from nothing but where new connections are made. Ideas that had not been previously associated with one another are put together and a new idea or theory emerges. Koestler terms this process 'bisociation'.

'Haha' refers to the fact that humour works because it puts together or makes a connection between two previously unconnected ideas. These may be puns (or play on words) such as the joke about what kind of pizza Father Christmas likes. Answer: deep and crisp and even (deep-pan, crisp and even). But humour can of course also operate on many different levels. Koestler suggests that 'the humorist ...deliberately chooses discordant codes of behaviour'. This is perhaps why satire works so well – it sets out to be disturbing. Koestler adds that 'all original comic invention is a creative act, a malicious discovery'.

The 'ah' reaction is described by Koestler as the opposite to laughter. It describes the emotions which are often described in the literature referring to early years curricula as awe and wonder. Freud called this emotion the 'oceanic' feeling and it is probably the emotion felt when in a state of what Csikszentmihalyi terms 'flow'. Koestler himself describes it as 'that expansion of awareness which one experiences on occasion in an empty cathedral when eternity is looking through the window of time, and in which the self seems to dissolve like a grain of salt in a lot of water'. (p649)

Mihaly Csikszentmihalyi (born 1934)

Csikszentmihalyi is currently probably the most quoted writer on the subject of creativity. He is an American and works at Claremont University in California. His name is particularly associated with the term 'flow'.

Flow is difficult to define but for Csikszentmihalyi it is the essential element of experiences which can be described as creative. He interviewed experts in a wide range of fields - people who devoted a lot of time and enthusiasm to a particular interest but who were not rewarded either financially or by public acclaim. He writes (16):

'It was clear from talking to them that what kept them motivated was the quality of experience they felt when they were involved with the activity..... it often involved painful, risky, difficult activities that stretched the person's capacity and involved an element of novelty and discovery. This optimal experience is what I have called "flow" because many of the respondents described the feeling when things were going well as an almost automatic, effortless, yet highly focused state of consciousness.'

Nine elements of flow are identified:

1. There are clear goals every step of the way.
2. There is immediate feedback to one's actions.
3. There is a balance between challenges and skills.
4. Action and awareness are merged.
5. Distractions are excluded from consciousness.
6. There is no worry of failure.
7. Self-consciousness disappears.
8. The sense of time becomes distorted.
9. The activity becomes rewarding just for its own sake.

Csikszentmihalyi uses the term 'autotelic' and it describes things we do for no other reason than because we enjoy the experience. Most things which we do are 'exotelic' – we do them for some later goal. Ideally Csikszentmihalyi suggests we should try to get flow from as many things as possible so that we feel that everything is worth doing for its own sake.

Ellis Paul Torrance (1915–2003)

Professor Torrance was best known for his pioneering research in the study of creativity. In 1974 he established the Torrance Tests of Creative Thinking and developed the Threshold Hypothesis which set out his view that creativity was not possible below a certain level of intelligence. His test built on Guilford's work and included simple tests of divergent thinking and other problem-solving skills. Scores were based on the number of relevant ideas produced; the range or categories of ideas; their originality and the amount of detail provided. In 1984, the University of Georgia where he worked established the Torrance Center for Creativity and Talent Development.

Edward de Bono (born 1933)

De Bono has been described as a polymath from Malta. Taking his first degree in Malta, he won a Rhodes scholarship to Oxford University. He was the first to introduce the term 'lateral thinking' and he has gone on to develop thinking about creativity in the world of business and currently runs very successful training courses in the world of business and education.

Comment

Creativity, as a concept, is currently of great interest in both commerce and education. It seems likely that those working in the early years have a particular responsibility to nurture it since it is closely linked to play and imagination. Young children cannot stop playing and they make more imaginative connections than at any other time in their lives. It is also the period when interests and enthusiasms are emerging. If we want children to develop particular expertise (as Csikszentmihalyi suggests is essential for the development of creative experts) then early childhood is the time to be nurturing positive attitudes to learning – through enjoyment and perseverance.

References

(1)   Ramachandran and Blakeslee (1999) Phantoms in the Brain *London: Fourth Estate*

(2)   Lewis-Williams, D. (2002) The Mind in the Cave *London: Thames and Hudson Ltd.*

(3)   Sternberg, R. (1988) (ed) The Nature of Creativity *Cambridge: Cambridge University Press*

(4)   Barron, F. (1988) 'Putting Creativity to Work' in Sternberg, R. (ed) The Nature of Creativity *Cambridge: Cambridge University Press (page 77)*

(5)   Freud 1959 quoted in Gardner, H. (1993) Creating minds *New York: Basic Books (page 24)*

(6)   Levitin, D. (2007) This is your brain on music *London: Atlantic Books*

(7)   Mihill 1993 cited in Pound, L. and Harrison, C. (2003)

(8)   Gardner, H. (1993) Creating minds *New York: Basic Books (page 24)*

(9)   Gardner, H. (1993) Creating minds *New York: Basic Books (see chapter 9 quote from pages 313-314)*

(10)   Barron, F. (1988) 'Putting Creativity to Work' in Sternberg, R. (ed) The Nature of Creativity *Cambridge: Cambridge University Press*

(11)   Guy Claxton (2006 BERA conference) refers to this as 'serendipity'.

(12)   Craft 2002 Singer and Singer, cited in Jenkinson, 2001: 58

(13)   Barron 1988 page 78 citing Burdick and Chevron

(14)   *Gardner, H. (2006)* Multiple Intelligences: New Horizons *New York; Basic Books*

(15)   *Bruce, T. (2004)* Cultivating Creativity in babies, toddlers and young children *London: Hodder and Stoughton*

(16)   *Csikszentmihalyi, M. (1997)* Creativity: flow and the psychology of discovery and invention *New York: HarperPerennial (page 110)*

Where to find out more

Bruce, T. (2004) Cultivating Creativity in babies, toddlers and young children *London: Hodder and Stoughton*

Csikszentmihalyi, M. (1997) Creativity: flow and the psychology of discovery and invention *New York: HarperPerennial*

Progressive twentieth century theories that shaped modern education

INTRODUCTION

Compulsory schooling began in 1870 but very soon reformers began to want to improve the system, making it more effective and in some cases more humane. Progressive reformers worked throughout the twentieth century and in this section some of their theories and the impact of those theories are examined.

KEY DATES

1850-1936
Edmond Holmes

1875-1925
Homer Lane

1883-1973
A. S. Neill

1885-1959
H. Caldwell Cook

1893-1974
Charlotte Buhler

1902-1987
Carl Rogers

1908-1970
Abraham Maslow

1923-1985
John Holt

The development of progressive twentieth century theories

The twentieth century saw immense changes in approaches to and thinking about education. The introduction of compulsory schooling in the latter part of the nineteenth century focused very much on the '3Rs'. It has been said that originally these were 'reading, writing and wroughting' (or being able to fashion things with your hands as in wrought iron), rather than 'reading, writing and 'rithmetic'. Whether or not this is true, there were also demands to create a literate population who would be more open to government requirements. Tax demands, for example, are much less effective if those receiving them cannot read.

The demand for a system of universal education also came from employers. The Industrial Revolution had meant that employers needed factory workers who did not need to be well-educated and often included children who provided cheap labour. However, as the nineteenth century progressed, it became apparent that the international trade which had developed meant that employers also needed clerks and book-keepers who could do sums, read and write.

By the beginning of the twentieth century many were dissatisfied with the system of education that had developed since 1870. There were many progressive thinkers who wanted to bring about change. In the sections that follow, the ideas about education and learning which developed throughout the twentieth century will be considered.

Working class poverty and educational reform

The poor quality of life of many impoverished and therefore unhealthy children and families led some reformers, such as the McMillan sisters (*How Children Learn* pages 23-25) and Maria Montessori (*How Children Learn* pages 29-31) to create schools that would alleviate the children's living conditions and improve their life chances. Both Maria Montessori (in Rome) and Margaret McMillan worked in city slum areas and developed strongly contrasting theories. The education developed by Montessori focused on practical tasks and sought to bring order and routine to children's lives. The McMillan sisters (working mainly in London and Bradford) favoured Froebel's ideas and highlighted the need to improve children's health and well-being through outdoor play and the provision of a rich and stimulating learning environment. Margaret McMillan believed that what was often regarded

Progressive twentieth century theories that shaped modern education

as low intelligence in young children often had its roots in the conditions in which they were forced to grow up. She considered that the nasal and respiratory complaints from which many suffered contributed to poor speech; being 'obliged to sit all day with their legs tucked under a table' (1) and that their 'fingers almost atrophied because they never had an opportunity to use them' (2). This led the sisters to the conclusion that educating the hand and nurturing the development of spoken language is the most important work of early education. They believed that their theories would lead to a new pedagogy, a new approach to learning and teaching.

Idealism before the Second World War

Two radical thinkers led the way. Edmond Holmes came first with the publication of a book in 1911 entitled *What is and What Might Be* which was to herald the progressive movement. He is said to have shocked many (see Key Figures in Idealism before the second world war below). He was followed by Homer Lane, an American who supported Freudian theories and was widely described as an extremist.

Then came Montessori (see *How Children Learn* pages 29-31) who is described as bringing 'things back into the realm of the possible and nearly normal, to show that what wilder spirits had preached could be practised, even in the large classes of the elementary school' (3). Although closely linked to these two extremists who were seeking to reform education in England, Montessori was regarded as the acceptable face of progressivism. She too had a powerful personality but because she was a doctor she was somehow regarded as more respectable. When she used words such as 'freedom' or 'independence' they seemed less threatening although it is clear that she was no less dedicated to reform of the education system.

In the period between the two world wars, other reformers such as Rudolf Steiner (*How Children Learn* pages 26–28) and Susan Isaacs (*How Children Learn* pages 32–35) began to set up what were regarded as progressive models of education. This progressivism often focused on children who were not poor, but in fact rather affluent. The work of these progressives arose out of dissatisfaction with existing approaches to education. In fact, like Margaret McMillan, they wanted to establish a new way of learning and teaching. Their work was often fuelled by the growing understanding of psychoanalytic theories (*How Children Learn* pages 17–20). Three key words characterise progressive approaches to education during this period – namely individuality, freedom and growth (4). The approaches also reflected the optimism felt by many educators and public alike as the First World War

KEY DATES

1926-2002
Ivan Illich

1967
Publication of the Plowden Report

1975
Publication of the Bullock Report

ended. This of course was not to last, as the Second World War loomed on the horizon.

It is interesting to consider that many of these radical approaches were often intended to run throughout childhood. However, although they have become widely accepted in the early years, their theories are rarely apparent in work with older children. Margaret McMillan's school for example catered initially for children from two to nine years of age. 'She saw her principles as applicable to older children... the nursery... merely made a right beginning possible' (5).

There are exceptions to this. Many Steiner schools cater for the full age range, although they do generally have a higher proportion of younger children. Summerhill, established in 1921 by Alexander Neill, remains a boarding school, catering for children throughout the years of schooling but understandably not catering for very young children.

Key figures in idealism before the Second World War

Edmond Holmes (1850-1936)

The publication of Edmond Holmes' book *What is and What might be* in 1911 is said to mark the beginning of progressive educational thinking in England (5). Holmes had been the Chief Inspector for elementary schools right up until the year of his book's publication, but claimed that he had done 'as much mischief in the field of education as (he) possibly could' (6). The book was based on the work of a school in Sussex and in order to make the school anonymous Holmes referred to it as Utopia. He further claimed that it offered schooling in which children could feel free and joyful – which he contrasted with the 'blind, passive, literal, unintelligent obedience... on which the whole system of Western education has been reared' (7).

The publication of this book occurred at a time when there was widespread criticism of the education system. There was agreement about the need for change but wide-ranging disagreement about the direction that change should take. Play and children's interests began to be talked about as a focus for learning and teaching.

There was, however, even tension between those we would now identify as having similar goals. Margaret McMillan, for example, believed she had nothing in common with Montessori; Susan Isaacs (*How Children Learn* pages 32–35) disagreed vehemently with Piaget (*How Children Learn* pages 36–38). (Paradoxically, Piaget made no claim to be an educational reformer, but he was to have a strong influence on developments in education after the second world war.)

Homer Lane (1875–1925)

It is suggested that Homer Lane provided a role model for A.S.Neill when he was setting up Summerhill School. Only someone as courageous as Neill would have felt able to act on such an example, since Lane has been described as extravagant and 'too extreme to act as a model' (8). He is variously described as determined to excel, ebullient, unpredictable and restless. In fact Lane is reported to have described himself as 'the only man who really understood the message of Jesus Christ' (9).

Lane was American, born in New Hampshire. He had had some remarkable results in working with young delinquent boys and when he visited England in 1912, he was invited by the Earl of Sandwich to set up a co-educational community which was to be called the Little Commonwealth. Lane had an unfaltering belief that giving difficult children freedom and trust would result in a community of order and authority. The results he achieved astonished many. A contemporary, Elsie Bazeley, said that the Little Commonwealth allowed progressives to see their ideals or convictions achieved (10), even though the school was only open for a short period of time. The Earl of Lytton described the community as proving that something believed to be unattainable could be achieved in practice (11).

Alexander Sutherland Neill (1883–1973)

Best known as the founder of Summerhill School, a progressive school renowned to this day as the school where children did not have to attend lessons, Neill and his writing have influenced the development of education in this country.

Neill was the son of a teacher and began his working life as a teacher in the state sector. He was unhappy about the education offered to children and in 1921 opened Summerhill School, which embodied many of the progressive ideas prevalent among thinkers and academics at that period. He wrote a number of books. Some, such as *Summerhill*, were specifically about his school and its work. Others such as *The Problem Child* (1927), *The Problem Family* (1949), and *The Problem Parent* (1949) were more general texts. Central to his beliefs was the idea that the happiness of the child was of paramount consideration in the child's upbringing and that this happiness grew from a sense of personal freedom in the child. He felt that deprivation of this sense of freedom during childhood and all the consequent unhappiness experienced by the repressed child was responsible for most of the psychological disorders of adulthood. A Freudian, Neill was strongly opposed to sexual repression and the imposition of the strict Victorian values of his childhood era. This idea was controversial at the time, but even today the school has many critics and has often been reported as being in conflict with OFSTED. Most recent OFSTED reports of the school, now run by Neill's daughter, have been favourable.

Neill felt that Summerhill School showed that, free from the coercion of traditional schooling, children and young people learned to develop their own motivation and did not act in the self-indulgent ways that adults might predict. He felt that children who attended Summerhill were likely to emerge with a healthy and mature scepticism towards adult society. The achievements of those attending the school were perhaps all the more remarkable considering that the children accepted by Summerhill were often from problematic backgrounds, where parental conflict or neglect had resulted in children arriving in a particularly unhappy state of mind. The school remains committed to democracy. Children are not compelled to attend lessons, meetings are held to determine school rules and pupils have equal voting rights with school staff.

H. Caldwell Cook (1885–1939)

Caldwell Cook's influence in the progressive movement came from a book he published in 1917 which was entitled *The Play Way*. He had completed it in 1915, reputedly in a great hurry since he feared that the war would make it impossible for his message to be spread. He declared that 'the one thing upon which my heart is fixed is to make this dream come true in this our England' (12). It is important to remember that he was seeking to spread play-based approaches right through the secondary school, not merely within the primary school.

Key themes in the book echoed the views of other progressive thinkers with an emphasis on learning rather than teaching; joy; activity, interest and democracy. Caldwell Cook was renowned as a man of great commitment. He wrote that:

'it must have occurred to every one that since a child's life under his own direction is conducted all in play, whatever else we want to interest him in should be carried on in that medium, or at the very least connected with play as closely as possible' (13).

The third force: the emergence of humanistic psychology

The end of the Second World War in 1945 brought a period of renewed optimism. The 1944 Education Act set up a three tier system of secondary education (grammar schools; technical schools and secondary modern schools). It was believed that it would be possible to offer teaching which more closely matched the learning needs of children – a debate which continues to this day, with talk of personalised learning and individual tuition.

Groups of psychologists at that time began to reject both behaviourism (see 'Burrhus Skinner and behaviourism' in *How Children Learn* page 42) and the psychoanalytic theories of Freud and his followers (see 'Sigmund Freud and psychoanalytic theories' in *How Children Learn* page 17) in favour of what they termed a 'Third Force', generally known as humanistic psychology.

The most famous of those leading this new movement were perhaps Abraham Maslow, Carl Rogers, and Charlotte Buhler (who came to be known as the mother of humanistic psychology). Two meetings were held in the late 1950s in Detroit. Those who attended were interested in setting up a professional group in order to focus on broad topics such as self-actualization, health, creativity, being, becoming and individuality. In 1961, this movement was formally launched as the American Association for Humanistic Psychology.

Key figures in humanistic psychology

Charlotte Buhler (1893–1974)

Charlotte Buhler was born in Berlin – her father an architect, her mother a musician. When she was still at school she expressed an interest in studying psychology. Her teacher's retort that psychology was not about people but about sensory reactions is said (14) to have stimulated her interest in what has become known as 'humanistic psychology'.

Because one of Buhler's parents was Jewish, she and her family were in grave danger during the Nazi regime in Germany and Austria where she was working. In 1938 while Charlotte was in England her husband was arrested. She was eventually able to secure work for both of them and in 1940 they were accepted as refugees in America.

Charlotte's work before and after this period focused on observations of children, from which she was able to make a strong contribution to understanding of child development.

In her work Buhler had inspired many women to study at a time when women were still not seen as being capable of academic work. Similarly, although Rogers and Maslow are frequently referred to as the fathers of this third force, Buhler's ideas are said to have pre-dated theirs. She is widely described as the mother of humanistic psychology.

Carl Rogers (1902–1987)

Rogers was born in Chicago, the fourth of six children. He worked closely with Buhler and Maslow and in 1964 was elected 'humanist of the year'. Some of his early work was with neglected and abused children. Rogers is probably best known for his contribution to psychotherapy and, working with his daughter, he developed the person-centred approach to therapy. His influence in education and training hinges around his view of 'positive regard'. Those brought up in a climate of unconditional positive regard can achieve self-actualization or fulfilment while those who receive only conditional love find it more difficult to have a sense of worth – needing always to live up to other people's expectations.

Abraham Maslow (1908–1970)

Maslow is perhaps the best-known of this group because of his work on self-actualization and the hierarchy of needs. An American, born in Brooklyn, Maslow was the eldest of seven children. His work is regarded as innovative because he looked not at the mentally ill or disturbed, as many other psychologists did, but at those whom he considered to have achieved self-actualization of growth needs.

The hierarchy which Maslow identified was that bodily needs and the need for safety and security or love and esteem must be met before humans can go on to seek fulfilment. In his early versions of this theory, he omitted cognitive and aesthetic needs – perhaps otherwise described as far back as Socrates as a need for truth and beauty. This work continues to have a strong influence in management training.

Deschoolers and their theories

By the 1960s, the idealism which had been so prevalent at the end of the Second World War had begun to fade. All those who had seen the end of the war as a time to develop a more equal society began to become disillusioned. The school system was not living up to the ideals that had been so widely held. During the 1960s and 1970s a wide range of writers, mainly American, published books calling for 'deschooling' (15). Some of these writers called for the abolition of formal schooling. These became a focus for home schooling groups such as Education Otherwise. Other theorists and writers argued for a radical rethink of the ways in which schools are organised and what their purpose is thought to be.

Key figures in the deschooling movement

Ivan Illich (1926–2002)

Illich was born in Vienna, Austria and studied in Rome and Salzburg. In 1951 he moved to New York, where he served as a priest in a community with high numbers of Irish and Puerto Rican parishioners. In 1956 he became vice-rector at the Catholic University in Puerto Rico. Throughout his life his focus has been on Latin America. It is from this perspective that his dissatisfaction with the role that education and other public institutions were playing in the lives of poor people that his work has grown. His most famous publication is Deschooling Society which was first published in 1971. This had been preceded (although published in English at the same time) by a book entitled Celebration of Awareness: a call for institutional revolution.

John Holt (1923–1985)

Holt has been described as the grandfather of the deschooling and homeschooling movements in North America. He wrote a number of influential books in the 1960s, the most famous of which are probably *How Children Fail*, *How Children Learn* and *Instead of Education* (16). His writing chimes well with the psycholinguists who favoured whole language approaches to literacy and to related demands for apprenticeship approaches to education. These theories themselves, of course, owe much to the work of Vygotsky (*How Children Learn* pages 39–41).

Research and theory-led teaching

The final years of the twentieth century saw some interesting and often conflicting ideas about learning and education. In 1967 the Plowden Report was published. It was strongly influenced by the work of Piaget and contained the memorable phrase 'at the heart of the educational process lies the child'. It made the case for positive discrimination in favour of schools in areas of socio-economic deprivation, where teachers were to be better paid than those working in more affluent areas. It also placed a strong emphasis on the involvement of parents in their children's education.

The Bullock Report, published in 1975, focused on language learning and teaching. It placed a similar emphasis on the role of parents. It included the words 'the best way to prepare the very young child for reading is to hold him on your lap and read aloud to him stories he likes, over and over again'. The publication of this report coincides with and influenced many of the innovations in the teaching of reading and writing which occurred during the 1980s and 1990s.

In 1976 the Prime Minister, James Callaghan, referred to the secret garden of the curriculum. There was renewed interest in what should be taught and this was to lead to what has been called the Great Debate. In time this led to the introduction of the first National Curriculum in the late 1980s. Although the government of the day claimed that teaching would be left to teachers, it was not long before the literacy and numeracy strategies were set out for primary schools describing in minute detail how reading, writing and mathematics should be taught.

This focus on both the 'what' and 'how' of learning quickly spread to the early years curriculum. The first step was the publication in 1996 of the *Desirable Learning Outcomes*. This was followed in 2000 by the *Curriculum Guidance for the Foundation Stage*, *Birth to Three Matters* in 2002 and then by the Early Years Foundation Stage guidance to be implemented in 2008.

Alongside these policy developments there has been a large amount of research and the development of wide ranging theories about learning and teaching. There are many difficulties in designing, carrying out and interpreting the findings of research projects. There are many different views about what education is about. Is it simply about making children literate and numerate as quickly as possible? What about computer literacy? Or emotional literacy? Or visual literacy? Is it about developing creativity? Is it about social and emotional well-being? Or good attitudes to learning? Of course, as early years practitioners you are likely to say that it is about all these things. But sometimes in trying to focus on one aspect of education practitioners can unwittingly undermine another. For example, if learning to read becomes a terrible chore and children cease to be interested in reading, then their disposition to learn may be undermined.

There are of course different views about how learning occurs, or even what it is. Those who believe that it is primarily about memorising will favour a different approach to education to those who believe that learning is mainly about problem-solving. Behaviourists (like Skinner – see *How Children Learn* pages 42–43) hold very different views from the humanistic psychologists introduced earlier in this section. Neuroscience (see 'Research into brain development' in *How Children Learn* pages 76–78) has taught us a great deal about learning, but there remain many things that we do not know about the processes involved. We know that memory plays a part; as do motivation, persistence and social context. What we don't know is what will be needed in the future – perhaps this is why there is so much current interest in creativity. It may be that helping children to build flexible and creative brains is our best hope.

Perhaps a major factor to consider in evaluating research projects is the extent to which short-term gains in attainment may get in the way of long-term achievements. The early start to formal schooling which exists in this country 'isn't as impressive as one might imagine. If anything, the evidence suggests that our children are disadvantaged by starting school earlier than their international peers.... International studies show that children who enter school later do better at reading' (17). In the section that follows the focus will be on two contrasting approaches to evaluating and developing effective learning and teaching by theorists and researchers who share an aim to improve the quality of education.

The Effective Provision of Pre-School Education (EPPE) Project (1997-2003)

Profile
The EPPE project is a government-funded longitudinal study which set out to compare the effects of different types of pre-school experience. The study is currently tracking children entering secondary schools who were first studied when they were in pre-school education.

Background
The rationale for the EPPE project arose out of the education grant which was offered to pre-school settings following the introduction initially of the Desirable Learning Outcomes and then the Curriculum Guidance for the Foundation Stage. The government felt a need to weigh up which of the many diverse approaches to education in the early years were most cost-effective. They commissioned a team of eminent researchers led by Professor Kathy Sylva at Oxford University and Professor Iram Siraj-

Blatchford from the Institute of Education in London. This project attempts to identify the factors that have contributed to children's attainment and achievement.

Focus

The study aimed to track over 3000 children in order to:
- provide details and the impact of their pre-school experiences;
- identify the characteristics of different forms of pre-school provision which contribute to their effectiveness.

The influence of EPPE findings

This rich longitudinal study has offered a number of important findings. Among the most influential are:
- evidence of sustained shared thinking and its impact on achievement;
- findings on the impact of qualified/graduate teachers working in pre-school settings;
- findings on the impact that parents can have on their children's learning, regardless of their own level of education or social class.

Comment

This vast study has provided and continues to provide a huge amount of data about children's learning. The findings about the quality of different forms of pre-school provision have been controversial and have not always informed government policy in the way that might have been hoped.

Where to find out more

www.ioe.ac.uk/schools/ecpe/eppe/eppe/eppeaims.htm
www.ioe.ac.uk/schools/ecpe/eppe/eppe3-11/eppe3-11aims.htm

Building Learning Power (BLP)

Profile

BLP aims to make children more effective learners by identifying the learning dispositions that will make them lifelong learners.

Background

Guy Claxton who established this approach is a psychologist. He was formerly involved in teacher education but now works with established teachers, developing approaches to learning. He lectures extensively and works in a variety of local authorities.

Focus

Claxton has identified four strands that children need to develop in order to be effective learners (see table on the following page). The four strands are resilience, resourcefulness, reflection and making relationships (or what he terms reciprocity in order to be able to identify 4Rs – but don't be put off by the language). The following table identifies the qualities which contribute to each of the four strands of effective learning.

The influence of Guy Claxton

It is difficult to judge just how strong the influence of this work is since Claxton is not alone in calling for a stronger emphasis on dispositions for learning. This is also true of the deschoolers (see page 64); theorists advocating whole language approaches to literacy; Ferre Laevers' work on well-being and involvement; Margaret Carr, one of the authors of Te Whariki (see How Children Learn pages 67-69); and the EYFS. However, it is clear that the flexible and creative approaches he advocates are in line with much current thinking.

Comment

There is some tension between government policies which recognise the need for flexible and creative learners and those which seek to return to old approaches to learning and teaching with more imposed structure and less room for beginning with what the learner already knows. Policy seems to be attempting to look in both directions like a two-headed pantomime horse! The Great Education Debate introduced by Callaghan has not resolved this conflict.

Where to find out more

http://www.buildinglearningpower.co.uk/blp/Home.html
http://www.guyclaxton.com/blp.htm

Progressive twentieth century theories that shaped modern education

RESILIENT	RESOURCEFUL	REFLECTIVE	RECIPROCAL (making relationships)
Curious (proactive)	Questioning (how come?)	Clear thinking (logical)	Collaborative (team member)
Adventurous (up for a challenge)	Open-minded ('negative capability')	Thoughtful (where else could I use this?)	Independent (can work alone)
Determined (persistent)	Playful (let's try...)	Self-knowing (own habits)	Open to feedback
Flexible (trying other ways)	Imaginative (could be)	Methodical (strategic)	Attentive (to others)
Observant (details/patterns)	Integrating (making links)	Opportunistic (serendipity)	Empathic (other people's feelings)
Focused (distractions)	Intuitive (reverie)	Self-evaluative (how's it going?)	Imitative (contagious)

(adapted from Guy Claxton 2006 BERA conference Building learning power)

Comment

The twentieth century has been a time of immense change and the twenty-first century looks likely to be a period of even greater change in education. Learning about learning has increased and developed and the themes that the early idealists evoked - namely individuality, freedom and growth - keep returning. As we learn more from neuroscience and learn to trust our professionalism, it looks likely that the debate will continue.

References

(1)   McMillan, M. (1923) Education Through the Imagination Sonnenschein (page 34)

(2)   Whitbread, N. (1975) The Evolution of the Nursery-Infant School London: Routledge and Kegan Paul

(3)   Selleck, R. (1972) English Primary education and the Progressives, 1914-1939 London: Routledge and Kegan Paul (page 30)

(4)   Selleck, R. (1972) English Primary education and the Progressives, 1914-1939 London: Routledge and Kegan Paul

(5)   Selleck, R. (1972) English Primary education and the Progressives, 1914-1939 London: Routledge and Kegan Paul

(6)   Selleck, R. (1972) English Primary education and the Progressives, 1914-1939 London: Routledge and Kegan Paul (page 24, citing Holmes)

(7) *Selleck, R. (1972)* English Primary education and the Progressives, 1914-1939 *London: Routledge and Kegan Paul (page 23, citing Holmes)*

(8) *Selleck, R. (1972)* English Primary education and the Progressives, 1914-1939 *London: Routledge and Kegan Paul (page 28)*

(9) *Selleck, R. (1972)* English Primary education and the Progressives, 1914-1939 *London: Routledge and Kegan Paul (page 26)*

(10) *Selleck, R. (1972)* English Primary education and the Progressives, 1914-1939 *London: Routledge and Kegan Paul*

(11) *Selleck, R. (1972)* English Primary education and the Progressives, 1914-1939 *London: Routledge and Kegan Paul*

(12) *Caldwell Cook, H. (1917)* The Play Way *London: William Heinemann (page 2)*

(13) *Caldwell Cook, H. (1917)* The Play Way *London: William Heinemann (page 10)*

(14) *Ragsdale, S. Charlotte Malachowski Buhler, Ph.D. (1893-1974) http://www.webster.edu/~woolflm/charlottebuhler.html*

(15) *Hern, M. (1996)* Deschooling our Lives *Gabriola Island, BC: New Society Publishers (page 27)*

(16) *Holt, J. (1964)* How Children Fail *New York: Pitman*
Holt, J. (1967) How Children Learn *New York: Delacourt*
Holt, J. (1976) Instead of Education *Boston; Holt Associates*

(17) *Harker, L. (2007)* 'School must start at seven' The Guardian *December 12th*

Where to find out more

Hern, M. (1996) Deschooling our Lives *Gabriola Island, BC: New Society Publishers*

Holt, J. (1976) Instead of Education *Boston: Holt Associates*

Neill, A. S. (1968) (first published 1926) Summerhill *Harmondsworth, Middx: Pelican Books*

The development of theories about how children learn to talk

INTRODUCTION

Learning to talk is probably the most effective piece of learning we do in the course of our lives. Language is not only a vital element of our everyday lives, but a crucial aspect of thinking and learning. Although we now know much more about how language is learnt, it remains a miraculous process.

1904-1990
Burrhus Skinner
(Pennsylvania USA)

1924-2000
Basil Bernstein

1926-1972
Roger Brown

1928
Noam Chomsky's birth

1959
Publication of Chomsky's paper Review of "Verbal Behaviour" by B.F. Skinner

1962
Publication of Ruth Weir's influential study Language in the Crib

Developing theories of how children learn to talk

Burrhus Skinner, the best known of the behavioural theorists (see *How Children Learn* page 43), held the view that language was learnt through reward. This behaviourist view was strongly challenged by Noam Chomsky, an American professor of linguistics. Chomsky developed an early interest in language, probably fostered by his father's research into Hebrew grammar. Chomsky remains a respected philosopher with wide interests including politics and education.

The view that Chomsky put forward in 1959, early in his career (1), was to have a widespread influence on views of language learning throughout the second half of the twentieth century. Chomsky suggested that far from being a process of learning entirely shaped by conditioning, as Skinner suggested, language learning was actually driven by innate or inborn forces. He put forward the theory that language learning in humans is driven by a Language Acquisition Device (often known as a LAD) which enables even young children to understand the rules of language. This theory is described as nativist, meaning that it is inborn, owing more to nature than to nurture. It emphasises a 'Universal Grammar' or a system built into the human brain which underpins all human languages (2). It was LAD, claimed Chomsky, which made it possible to learn the very complex and abstract rules of a language relatively quickly. The huge leaps which children make in the two years from two to four years of age would not be possible, he claimed, without the existence of such a structure in the brain.

The ensuing debate between Skinner (who believed that language learning came about through social conditioning) and Chomsky (who believed that the apparatus which enables humans to be successful language users is innate) was to lead to the development of a wide range of theories about the way in which language is acquired or developed. These can be broadly put into four distinct groups or categories (3) which together show the ways in which thinking about language have developed.

Focus on the grammar of language

Initially, Chomsky's arguments led to an interest in the grammatical structures of language. While Chomsky's theory identified what is learnt in becoming a competent language user, it did nothing to explain how this learning occurred (4). Amazing as this may seem in the twenty-first century, this research, which began to explore how speech and language development occurs, was made possible by the development of portable tape recorders. Being able to play and replay examples of children's speech made it possible to analyse and describe the rules and assumptions by which children in the early stages of language learning were operating.

Chomsky's argument for innate understanding of the structures of language was supported by research originally carried out in the 1950s, but is widely replicated to this day. The experiment is commonly known as the 'Wug Test' (5). In order to ensure that the words being used in the experiment are not known to some of the children but not others, so-called 'nonce' or made-up words are used. The researcher makes a statement to children which allows them to demonstrate, in answering, their understanding of the structures of language.

So for example, the researcher may say that the object she is showing a child is a wug. When showing another of these objects, he or she will say 'now I have two...?', leaving a gap for the child to say 'wugs'. A similar test is used in order to demonstrate that children understand the rule for making verbs refer to the past tense. So the researcher may say something like 'Every day I gorp, so yesterday I ...?', expecting and usually receiving the child's response to be 'gorped'.

Of course in young children's everyday speech we hear examples of their use (and sometimes overuse) of grammatical rules. When a young child says 'I goed' or 'I saw two mouses' they are showing that they know the rules but that they have over-generalised them, assuming that all nouns or verbs behave in the same way. Sometimes they then go on to acknowledge the irregular forms ('went' and 'mice') but still applying the regular rule, in which case you may hear children saying 'wented' or 'mices'.

One of the best-known theorists researching the development of grammar was Roger Brown. During the 1960s, he and colleagues collected examples of children's natural speech. This enabled them to identify the sequence in which grammatical structures were learned and used by young children. His research was not published until 1973, when it began to strongly influence views of children's language learning.

Brown devised a method of analysing the complexity of children's talk, which he called the Mean Length of Utterance (MLU). MLU records not only the number of words which children use in any phrase or sentence but the complexity of the words used. For example (6) 'Daddy eat red apple' would give an MLU of four (one for each word), whereas 'Daddy eats apples' would

KEY DATES

1973
Publication of A First Language by Roger Brown

1975
Publication of Learning to Mean by Halliday

score a value of five (one for each of the three words plus one for each of the grammatically correct addition of 's' to 'eats' and 'apples'). Brown's work demonstrated that, between the ages of two and four, children's MLU went from two (for example 'Where mummy?') to an average of eight or more (for example 'When is mummy coming home from work?')

At around the same time as Roger Brown was conducting his research on young children's use of grammar, another American, Daniel Slobin, was undertaking research which also took Chomsky's theories as its starting point. Unlike Chomsky, who took adults' use of grammar as a benchmark for development, Slobin, working over many years, looked at the ways in which children speaking different languages developed what he called 'child grammar' (7). Chomsky put forward the theory that children somewhat passively obey Universal Grammar throughout their linguistic development, Slobin, working from the language that children produce, attempts to understand the thought processes underpinning that development. He suggests that the child constructs their own understanding of the rules of grammar from their unique language environment.

The links between language, learning and thinking

The link between language and thinking will be considered in two distinct ways. Firstly there is research about language development. This emphasises the way in which the developing brain operates in relation to language, in precisely the same way as it does with everything else that is experienced. This has been described as 'bootstrapping' – using all available evidence and using all known connections in order to make sense or meaning. Secondly the key that language offers to developing thinking will be examined.

The use of the term 'bootstrapping' (8) is most readily to be found in the work of Steven Pinker. Other theorists (9) suggest that bootstrapping may happen as a result of children learning the prosody (or tune of language) or gaining awareness of the structure of language. An example of the former can be seen when children use whole phrases almost as though they were a single word – for example 'please may I have a ...?', 'all gone' or 'give it to mummy'.

Pinker, however, argues for something called semantic bootstrapping, suggesting that children use known meanings in order to make more meanings. He writes that in order to learn language, children must first have learned a lot of nouns – the names of things in their environment (which carry the most information) – such as cats, dogs, toys, cups, plates and biscuits. Having done this, his theory is that the young child can make sense of sentences such as 'give daddy the ball'. Since daddy and ball are known concepts they can be used as a key (or bootstrap) to understanding the unknown elements of the sentence.

There are many possible criticisms of this theory. One major one is that Pinker's view does not take account of development in other languages and cultures. There is evidence (10) that there are strong cultural differences in the way in which language is learnt. The emphasis in Western societies appears to be on teaching nouns, as things which can be grouped and classified. In Eastern cultures the world is structured more in terms of actions. So for example, an English-speaking parent will say something like 'there's a doggy' or 'see the cow', while Korean-speaking mothers use more verbs. These linguistic differences can be seen to make differences in development. In the study referred to, Korean-speaking children were able to solve problems such as using a stick or other object to reach a toy earlier than English-speaking children. Children growing up with English as their first language were able to categorise or sort objects earlier.

These ideas link closely to ideas that were discussed in an earlier section of this book, Ancient theories that shaped modern thinking about learning. They also link to something that is known as the Sapir-Whorf hypothesis which claims that the language we learn shapes the way we perceive reality and think about it. Although the idea as put forward by Edward Sapir and his student Benjamin Whorf has been criticised, it continues to influence thinking about thought and language. Many people continue to believe that the grammar or vocabulary of the language we use influences the way in which we think. The findings detailed above about language learning seem to suggest that the way in which babies are introduced to language also influences their thinking. However this does not mean that they are unable to think in different ways (11), merely that they are most likely to absorb the things that those around them are interested in.

Many writers and theorists have alluded to the link between language and thinking. There has been widespread debate about the role of language in learning to think. As discussed in *How Children Learn* (see page 40) Piaget and Vygotsky held different views about the relationship between thought and language. While Vygotsky believed that language supported the development of conceptual understanding, Piaget believed that relevant language could only be used once a concept had been formed. One largely consistent view is that language is a tool for thinking and as such is best developed in meaningful contexts. Indeed, the 'development of the language of thought is fostered more by interacting with a knowledgeable person than by studying books or attending classes and exhibits' (12).

Among the best-known of the theorists was Lois Bloom (13), a colleague of Roger Brown. She drew attention to the fact that complex cognitive ideas may be contained in children's limited verbal output. She referred to the fact that the 'context of utterance' gave a key to what the young child wanted to say, that in fact toddlers and young children are able to mean more than they can readily say or communicate. Using the example of a child saying 'mummy-sock', the child (depending on the context of the conversation) may mean

Mummy is wearing socks
Mummy is not wearing socks
Mummy, where is my sock?
Mummy, the sock has fallen on the floor
Mummy is putting on my socks.

The importance of social contexts for language learning and use

The influence of the work of Piaget throughout the 1960s probably meant that the interpersonal and social uses of language and communication were overlooked. Piaget's focus was not social, but logical and mathematical. Research that emerged in the 1970s and 1980s challenged Piaget's view that young children are egocentric (see *How Children Learn* pages 37-38). As one book stated in 1985 (14) 'perhaps (children) only appear to be so if the observing adult does not engage in an interpersonal relationship with them.'

Some of the most influential writing at this time came from Halliday (15) who collected and analysed the speech or utterances of his young son Nigel. Unlike Bloom, Halliday included cries and coos as well as the use of developing recognisable words in identifying seven different functions for which language is used. The table below describes the uses of language which were identified by Halliday, attributing meaning to the utterances of the youngest children (16):

Function identified by Halliday:	Description	Example
The instrumental function	Language is used to get something for the speaker. It is called instrumental because the voice is used as an extension or instrument of the hand	I want.... I need....
The regulatory function	Language is used to get somebody else to do something	Stop that Do that again
The interactional function	Language is used to build a sense of closeness or group membership between the speaker and listener(s)	You know?
The personal function	The speaker's feelings and attitudes are shared	I love you I'm sad
The heuristic function	Language is used to ask questions and find things out	What's that
The imaginative function	Language is used for the sheer fun of it – playing with sounds, rhythms and humour	Baa, baa black sheep
The representative function	Language is used to communicate facts and convey information. Reality is represented with words	It's snowing

Jerome Bruner (see *How Children Learn* pages 47-49) has inspired a huge amount of research into language development. In response to Chomsky's LAD, Bruner suggested that language does not simply arise through the innate mechanisms of the brain, but through the way in which parent–child interactions shape children's communications. He made this idea memorable by terming it a Language Acquisition Support System (LASS) and states that 'it is the interaction between LAD and LASS that makes it possible for the infant to enter the linguistic community – and, at the same time, the culture to which the language gives access' (17).

Bruner was also responsible for drawing attention to the importance of the games which adults play with children for language development. These include turn-taking games (such as peek-a-boo) which allow children to play at taking turns which will be needed for conversation without the need to include the words. Similarly the songs and rhymes which adults typically use with babies allow them to rehearse the words and sounds and segments of language without the need for turn-taking.

The vital role of adults in supporting the development of language

Just as the development of audio recording supported researchers' growing interest in the development of grammar in young children, so the development of video recording has had a great impact on our understanding of the social aspects of language and communication. Bruner's view that mothers (or other significant adults) are vital in the development of language was supported by the work of Colwyn Trevarthen. He analysed recordings of the interactions of mothers and babies and came to the conclusion that mothers attribute meaning to their babies' apparently random gurgles. In acting as though the babies' babbling is intentional – that saying 'dadada' means daddy – the baby comes to understand that sounds can mean something. The shared experience of the sound and the sight of daddy (or cat, or teddy, or whatever the sounds are being used to focus on) leads to understanding. The 'proto-conversations' (18) that develop, in which mothers and babies take turns and make contributions, sound like real conversation and act as a learning ground for developing understanding of language.

The style of interaction that adults use with young babies – raising the pitch of their voices; emphasising parts of words; repeating words and syllables; and the use of songs and rhymes with a simple structure – is often known as 'motherese'. This does not mean that it is only mothers who use such a style. All adults and even very young children do.

It has been suggested that the human brain is hardwired (19) to support the development of language in babies. As babies babble, for example, adults respond by echoing the sounds the baby makes and then by raising and lowering the pitch at which the sounds were first made. This helps to create the sounds the baby first made as a joint focus – what psychologists call 'intersubjectivity'. The responses which adults make are too rapid to be anything other than reflex responses, which means that we have not learnt to interact with babies in particular ways but that we're born knowing.

Adults all around the world also use particular tunes to represent different feelings or emotions they wish to communicate to babies. So in telling babies how lovely they are or in trying to stop them scratching their faces, the sounds (but not the words themselves) we use will be very similar in different languages. Finally, the songs that are used with babies around the world have some common characteristics which further suggest that communication with babies is instinctive. The songs have similar rhythms, but have variations in tempo such as in This is the way the ladies ride, when each rider such as the gentleman or the old man, is sung at a different speed. The songs have a story-like structure which has a climax which invites an emotional response. Walking round the garden like a teddy-bear for example creates suspense with its 'one step, two step' and laughter with the ending 'tickling under there'.

The impact of language research on educational policy and thinking

The 1960s saw a surge of concern both in Britain and the United States for children who were failing in the school system. In this country, the end of the Second World War and the 1944 Education Act had led people to hope that a new beginning would ensure a better future for children. By the 1960s it was becoming clear that schools alone could not effect such social change. The focus in the United States was the belief that they were falling behind the Russians in the new emerging technologies (such as space travel) and a wish to raise levels of achievement amongst all children.

America introduced Head Start programmes. These were designed to prepare socio-economically deprived children so that they could take better advantage of schooling. High/Scope is undoubtedly the most famous and long-lasting of these (see How Children Learn pages 56–59).

In this country there was a strong focus on the way in which social class and family background (20) impacted on language use and thus educational achievement (21). The Newsom Report went so far as to say that 'there is much unrealised talent among these (working-class) boys and girls whose potential is masked by inadequate powers of speech and the limitations of home background'.

The good thing about this point of view is that it has stimulated a huge amount of research into language. The bad thing is that it represents a prejudice which has continued to influence policy and practice. The work of Basil Bernstein offers an excellent example of the way in which research findings can be distorted by prejudice or assumptions.

The work of Basil Bernstein

Throughout the 1960s Bernstein had been developing theories that introduced the idea that language use in everyday situations used either 'elaborated' or 'restricted' codes. In fact all of us use a restricted linguistic code in many parts of our lives. The unfinished sentences, grunts and gestures that pass as conversation amongst families or close friends represent a restricted code. Even the silences in these conversations are significant. Within elaborated codes, on the other hand, language is more context-free, less reliant on the social aspects of conversation. It has been described as the language of education and is more likely to involve argument and critical analysis.

Bernstein, a sociologist, believed that (22) it was the class system itself which limited people's access to an elaborated code because of the actions of more powerful groups. His work, however, was widely interpreted as meaning that the reason for the failure of working class children was the fact that they spoke a restricted code. In fact 'restricted code' came to be wrongly seen as meaning 'working class language'. This idea has been described (23) as a 'comforting notion' which 'spread much more rapidly in educational circles than do most theoretical ideas'.

In 1963, Bernstein produced a report for the Department of Education which focused on the importance of language in compensatory education. This was to contribute to the Plowden Report which was published in 1967. In this report nursery education was seen as being important in getting children ready to benefit from school, rather than primarily for the child's own good. It also placed a strong emphasis on greater levels of parental involvement and for the first time established educational priority areas.

Do schools disadvantage some children?

By the 1970s theorists had become uncomfortable with many of the ideas that underpinned compensatory education. Many began to ask whether it was schools themselves that created disadvantage. In 1971, Bernstein himself suggested that compensatory education implies 'that something is lacking in the family and so in the child' who in turn become 'little deficit systems'. He added somewhat bitterly that by harbouring such views, schools are led to feel that 'if only' working class parents 'were like middle class parents, then we could do our job' (24).

These views were both challenged and built on in America by Labov, whose focus was not on restricted code but on the use of non-standard dialects. He suggested that black children were being disadvantaged because teachers and researchers failed to recognise and value the non-standard forms being used by children and families. All too often, the different but systematic rules of non-standard speech were seen by teachers as laziness or sloppiness.

To summarize the impact of the work of both Labov and Bernstein, it would seem that both agreed that in order to fully understand the extent of children's linguistic competence it is necessary to talk about real things, things that are natural and known to children beyond the classroom context. Secondly, it seems very important to ensure that children are observed in conversation with people whom they regard as social equals and with whom they feel able to initiate conversation.

One particularly influential publication around this time was a research report by Douglas Barnes, James Britton and Harold Rosen (father of Michael Rosen the children's poet and laureate). In it, Rosen wrote (25):

'In children's encounter with the curriculum there is a confrontation between their comfortably acquired mother-tongue and the varieties of language which have grown up around institutionalized areas of learning. ... The speaking voice precedes the writing pen and the reading eye in the life-history of every normal child. ... Through improvised talk he can shape his ideas, modify them by listening to others, question, plan, express doubt, difficulty and confusion, experiment with new language and feel free to be tentative and incomplete. It is through talk that he comes nearer to others and with them establishes a social unit in which learning can occur and in which he can shape for public use his private and personal view. Thus we think that school learning should be so organized that pupils may use to the full their language repertoire and also add to it.'

Changing educational practice

The interest in whole language approaches to reading and writing which developed in the 1970s (described in the previous chapter The development of theories about how children learn to read and write) is closely linked to research and emerging theories about how children learn and use spoken language.

Two projects, in particular, were notable. Both were funded by the Schools Council and their results were published in 1973. The first was undertaken by Harold Rosen and his first wife Connie. This studied the use of language made by children at primary school and the relationship between language and thinking. The second was led by Joan Tough at the University of Leeds and was entitled 'Communication Skills in Early Childhood'. Although this emphasised the importance of one-to-one conversations between children and adults it was heavily biased towards the adults' input. Nevertheless, it did promote the idea that close attention to children's spoken language was a vital tool in understanding and promoting thinking and learning.

Early years research

In the 1980s, two highly significant research reports were published. Although they were very different kinds of research, and represented some different views about language, their findings included some remarkable similarities. Once again, emerging technology supported the research; this time it was small radio microphones worn by the children.

Young Children Learning

In 1984, Barbara Tizard and Martin Hughes published a book entitled *Young Children Learning*. It was a study of thirty girls, all four years old, who were attending a nursery school or class. Social class was established using a combination of the father's occupation and the mother's educational background. The language which the girls used at home with their mothers was compared to the language used at nursery. At that time the findings were controversial on a number of grounds. The authors suggested that all homes, including working class homes, provided rich learning environments. They provided an extensive range of experiences which have been shared by parent and child – leading to shared experiences or opportunities for the intersubjectivity referred to earlier in this section. In addition, each mother was only dealing with a small number of children, was engaging in real-life, meaningful activities such as cleaning, pegging out washing or writing to grandma, and, most importantly, had an intense and emotional relationship with her child.

Controversially, the researchers went on to describe the language learning environment provided by nursery staff as much less rich and stimulating than that found at home. They suggested that real-life experiences provided the best context for the kind of language that supported thinking and that play was not a helpful source for rich language. They went on to describe the difficulties faced by working-class girls in nursery schools and classes. In particular they found it difficult to produce the active, independent and exuberant language used at home within the institutional setting.

Tizard and Hughes are critical of the work of Joan Tough (described above) claiming that she paid insufficient attention to the social context offered by the home or the effect adults in school might have, particularly on working class children. They echo the work of Labov and Bernstein in writing (26) 'our study suggests that judgements on children's language abilities should be very tentative until a context is found where they talk freely and spontaneously. We suspect that the same caution should be exercised when pronouncing on other aspects of children's behaviour, such as their play.'

Bristol Language Development Study: the pre-school years
In 1985, Gordon Wells published the results of a longitudinal study which was carried out in Bristol. The language of 128 children aged from fifteen months to five years was collected over two and a quarter years and analysed. Wells' sample included both boys and girls and (unlike Tizard and Hughes) he found that both helping and play situations provided good opportunities for high level conversation. In particular, Wells identified characteristics of what he termed 'enabling homes'. The most important of these was undoubtedly motivation to talk. No attempts to engage the child worked unless the conversation was of intrinsic interest to him or her. Attempts to teach language directly met with little or no success, whereas conversations that were mutually pleasurable were successful in promoting thinking and language.

Wells describes (27) 'the child and the adult as (being) of equal importance but with roles that are complementary and interdependent. Responsibility for what is learned and for the order in which learning takes place rests almost entirely with the child'. He underlines the importance of Vygotsky's 'zone of proximal development' (see How Children Learn page 40). Adults (particularly parents) identify their child's language competence and gradually introduce new vocabulary or structures which will extend language use and understanding. Sometimes the child introduces a development of their own which parents build on in the same way.

Current concerns

In the twenty-first century, two important foci for language development have emerged. Wells' emphasis on the interactional nature of language has contributed to a strong feeling that children who are listened to are more likely to listen. In addition, the work of Eleanor Goldschmied and Dorothy Selleck published a decade later (28) highlighted the communicative competence of babies long before they could actually speak.

In 2001 Alison Clark and Peter Moss published a highly practical report entitled *Listening to Young Children*. This slim volume attempts to introduce a range of methods for tapping into children's meanings. Two years later Penny Lancaster and Vanessa Broadbent (working with Coram Family) produced a pack with the same title (*Listening to Young Children*) which looks at ways of listening through music, dance and art as well as more conventional means.

The EPPE project (see earlier section entitled Progressive twentieth century theories that shaped modern education) and the related REPEY research (29) drew attention to the importance of sustained shared thinking. These are conversations which involve a focus on a child's extended interest, described as a number of 'turns' in the conversation by some theorists. Both projects indicate that 'in the most effective early years settings staff provided (among other things) opportunities to sustain and challenge children's thinking and to model this for children to share sustained, shared thinking with other children.... Sustained interactions are possible with babies and young children and can cover both verbal and non-verbal communications' (30).

Standard versus regional or diverse English

Many policy documents on speaking and listening emphasise the need for children to use Standard English. Of course, children have a right to learn Standard English since it is both a nationally and internationally shared language – opening up opportunities in commercial, professional educational circles.

Standard English can only be effectively taught if children are able to see the links between their home register (or style of language use) and Standard English. Marian Whitehead reminds us that 'early childhood educators need to be particularly sensitive to the confusion, distress and lack of progress an excessive zeal for standard forms in talking and writing may produce.'

She continues by writing that 'children are closely bound to the accents and dialects of their homes and communities: very young children know no others and ?y associate the familiar voice and forms with deep affection and their closest ationships. Any outside criticism or rejection goes beyond language to become attack on the child and the home. The most damaging criticisms of all are the nspoken ones which small children pick up so quickly: raised eyebrows, grins, grimaces, shudders, physical recoil, pursed lips and averted gaze.'

Whitehead also reminds us that early years educators need to be clear about their personal stance on SE. Modelling the use of SE in everyday conversation and in the stories we share with children is probably the most effective way of helping them to use SE as part of their linguistic repertoire.

N.B. Standard English (SE) is not the same as Received Pronunciation (RP). SE refers to the form of the language and is effectively the kind of nglish which is used in written notices or books; it involves using complete ?ntences and standard grammar. RP is the voice or accent popularly iescribed as BBC English, but of course like all other forms of spoken 'anguage it is just another accent.
(based on Whitehead 2004 pages 31-33 and 100-103)

Story-telling and story-acting
Vivian Gussin Paley was an American kindergarten teacher who developed an approach to curriculum known as story-telling/story-acting. Children are given opportunities to tell their own stories which are written down in the exact form which the child uses to tell it. The stories are then acted out by the children. MakeBelieve Arts demonstrate the technique which they term ?licopter technique', taking the title from one of Paley's books *The Boy Who Would be a Helicopter*. They train early years practitioners to use the approach developed by Vivian Gussin Paley.

Although Paley retired many years ago, she continues to write gripping books about her work. During her working life, every day she transcribed her conversations with children and she uses these as the basis for reflections on her practice and the nature of children's learning, thinking and talking. Children's stories offer a window onto children's thinking, but some criticisms have focused on the fact that children's own words are used both in the story-writing and acting rather than standard English.

Bilingualism

Being a fluent speaker of more than one language is normal in many parts of the world. Very few communities are monolingual. Many children and adults are multilingual, being able to speak a variety of languages.

Simultaneous bilingualism refers to children who use two languages from birth, such as happens in families where mother and father both generally speak only their own first language with the child. This model is sometimes described as 'one language - one speaker'. Successive bilingualism occurs where children have grown up with their first language at home and then from about the age of three (perhaps when they start nursery) acquire additional languages.

Bilingualism is a positive asset. Advantages identified include increased self-esteem, positive sense of identity, positive attitudes towards language learning, increased problem-solving abilities and flexibility in thinking and greater awareness of the power of language. For this reason, children's home languages should be valued and not, explicitly or implicitly, undermined.

The mixing of languages and the switching of languages are powerful linguistic tools for the bilingual. These skills should not be misguidedly attributed to inadequate and partial language learning.

(based on Whitehead 2004 pages 45-46 and Siraj-Blatchford and Clarke 2000 page 30)

Cultural differences in how language is learnt

Throughout this section it may often appear that there is only one way to learn language. This is far from the case. Although many researchers describe the development of children brought up within western expectations and styles, some writers (such as Shirley Brice Heath and Bambi Schieffelin) describe language development in other cultures. They show us that even if adults do not use simplified language when speaking to children, they still learn to use language at much the same rate and in much the same way as in cultures where child-directed speech takes a particular form. In those cases language and socialisation are learnt as part of children's participation in everyday activities.

Mukherji and O'Dea suggest that nouns are acquired earlier than verbs but as seen earlier in the chapter (in the section entitled The links between language, learning and thinking) this appears not to be the case in all cultures.

The development of theories about how children learn to talk

Aspects of language development

Although language development is a very individual event, with every child going about it in different ways, there are some trends which can be identified. Different writers have identified different aspects of development. Just three ways of describing aspects of language development are shown here as examples of the ways in which some theorists, researchers and writers have set about the task.

Brown (1973)

Brown's study (described above) indicated that the shift from telegraphic speech to more complex grammar followed a distinct order:

Adding 'ing', eg. 'baby running'

Appearance of 'in' and 'on'

Adding 's' to plural nouns, eg. two cats

Use of irregular past tense, eg. 'daddy went work'

Addition of ''s' to show that something belongs to someone, eg. teddy's hat

Use of unshortened forms of the verb 'to be', eg. I am a good girl (not I'm a good girl); mummy is nice (rather than mummy's nice)

Use of 'a' and 'the', eg. I see the cat (rather than I see cat)

Use of regular past tense, eg. walked, jumped

Modifying regular verbs to take account of 3rd person, eg. baby dances (rather than baby dance)

Modifying irregular verbs, eg. daddy has hat on (rather than daddy hat)

Use of unshortened auxiliary verb, eg. he can go, I will like it

Use of shortened forms of verb 'to be', eg. I'm a good girl; mummy's nice

Use of shortened auxiliary verb eg we'll go home; I'd like a story.

Mukherji and O'Dea (2000)

0 to 12 months – described as pre-linguistic involves crying, cooing, babbling and the use of gestures.

12 to 18 months – described as one word stage.

18 to 30 months - described as the first sentences using stage one grammar. Sentences or utterances are likely to be simple, short and grammatical (although the grammar may not always be the grammar of adult speech). The speech of children at this stage is often described as telegraphic because they may omit words.

30 to 36 months – more complex sentences using stage two grammar. This may involve the use of grammatical markers such as plural forms of nouns (eg. adding 's') or past tense of verbs (eg. adding 'ed'). There is also likely to be some over-generalisation, which was described earlier in this section, and the early use of questions and negatives where the word order is often unconventional. When, for example, wanting to say 'I don't want to go to bed' the child may say 'go to bed no.'

Livingstone (2005) (based on page 235)

This author, drawing on the work of the television series *Child of our Time* has produced a checklist to help parents determine whether their two year olds, language development is satisfactory. She suggests that a two year old would be doing well to know all of the words in the first list and a third of the words in the second list, but much of this would depend on the child's experience.

First list

bye-bye	no	mummy/mum	cold	shoe
dog	juice	hug/cuddle	please	ouch/ow

Second list

tractor	car	book	milk	hat	thank you
cloud	rubbish	plate	towel	bed	settee/sofa
friend	person	hello/hi	shopping	carry	draw
find	rip/ tear	write	watch	gentle	fast
last	high	dry	after	day	this
where	all	some	need to	if	nose
school	fit	thirsty	our		

Comment

Language development is of vital importance to children's subsequent thinking, learning and achievement. Technology and neuroscience have contributed a great deal to our understanding of the processes involved, but there is still much that we don't understand. The privilege of both watching and contributing to the process which early years practitioners have is one to be cherished.

The development of theories about how children learn to talk

References

(1)   Chomsky, N. (1959) 'Review of "Verbal Behaviour" by B.F. Skinner' Language (35), cited by Nicholls, J. and Wells, G. (1985) 'Editors' introduction language and learning: an interactional perspective' In Wells, G. and Nicholls, J. (eds) Language and Learning: an interactional perspective. London: Falmer Press

(2)   Karmiloff, K. and Karmiloff-Smith, A. (2001) Pathways to Language London: Harvard University Press (page104)

(3)   Wells and Nicholls 1985, op cit

(4)   Karmiloff, K. and Karmiloff-Smith, A. (2001) Pathways to Language London: Harvard University Press (page111)

(5)   Berko-Gleason, J. (1958) 'The child's learning of English morphology' Word 14; 150-177

(6)   Karmiloff, K. and Karmiloff-Smith, A. (2001) Pathways to Language London: Harvard University Press (page101)

(7)   C. Ferguson and Slobin, D. (1973) (eds) Studies of Child Language Development Holt, Rhinehart and Winston and Slobin, D. (1985) (ed) The cross-linguistic study of language acquisition Vol 2: theoretical issues Lawrence Erlbaum Associates

(8)   Pinker, S. (1987) 'The bootstrapping problem in language acquisition' in McWhinney, B. (ed) Mechanisms of Language Acquisition Hillsdale, NJ: Erlbaum

(9)   Karmiloff, K. and Karmiloff-Smith, A. (2001) Pathways to Language London: Harvard University Press

(10)   Nisbett, R. E.(2004) The Geography of Thought London: Nicholas Brealey Publishing

(11)   Gopnik, A., Meltzoff, A., and Kuhl, P. (1999) How Babies Think London: Weidenfeld and Nicolson

(12)   Rogoff, B. (1990) Apprenticeship in Thinking Oxford: Oxford University Press (page 40, Rogoff citing John-Steiner)

(13)   Bloom, L. (1970) Language Development: form and function in emerging grammars Cambridge, Mass.: MIT Press

(14)   Wells, G. and Nicholls, J. (1985) Language and Learning: an interactional perspective London: Falmer Press (page 6)

(15)   Halliday, M. (1975) Learning how to Mean: explorations in the development of language London: Arnold

(16)   Based on Temple et al (1988) (2nd ed) The Beginnings of Writing London: Allyn and Bacon Inc.

(17)   Bruner, J. (1983) Child's Talk: learning to use language Oxford: Oxford University Press

(18)   Trevarthen, C. (1979) 'Communication and co-operation in early

infancy; a description of primary intersubjectivity' In Bullowa, M.
(ed) Before Speech Cambridge: Cambridge University Press

(19)   Papousek, H. and Papousek, M. (1994) 'Early musicality and
caregivers' infant-directed speech' In Deliege, I. (ed) Proceedings
of the 3rd International Conference for Music Perception
and Cognition Liege: ESCOM

(20)   Central Advisory Council for Education (1959) The Crowther Report

(21)   Central Advisory Council for Education (1963) The Newsom Report

(22)   Bernstein, B. (1971) Class, Codes and Control St. Albans Herts.:
Paladin

(23)   Nicholls, J. and Wells, G. (1985) 'Editors' introduction language and
learning: an interactional perspective' In Wells, G. and Nicholls,
J. (eds) Language and Learning: an interactional perspective.
London: Falmer Press (page 7)

(24)   Bernstein, B. (1971) Class, Codes and Control St. Albans Herts.:
Paladin

(25)   Rosen, H. (1969) 'Towards a language policy across the curriculum'
In Barnes, D., Britton, J. and Rosen, H. Language, the Learner and
the School Harmondsworth, Middx.: Penguin Education

(26)   Tizard, B. and Hughes, M. (1984) Young Children Learning London:
Fontana (page 258)

(27)   Wells, G. (1985) Language development in the pre-school years
Cambridge: Cambridge University Press

(28)   Goldschmied, E. and Selleck, D. (1996) Communication between
babies in their first year (video) London: National Children's Bureau

(29)   Effective Provision of Pre-school education (Siraj-Blatchford et al
2003) and Researching effective pedagogy in the early years
(Siraj-Blatchford et al 2002)

(30)   Dowling, M. (2005) Supporting Young Children's Sustained Shared
Thinking London: Early Education

Where to find out more

Clark, A. et al (2005) Beyond Listening: children's perspectives on early
childhood services Bristol: The Policy Press

Dowling, M. (2005) Supporting Young Children's Sustained Shared
Thinking London: Early Education

Whitehead, M. (2004) (3rd ed) Language and Literacy in the Early Years
London: Sage Publications